Thus we moved onward, through a day of gentle pleasure, feeling, as if we, alone, were the possessors, of this beautiful creation: for we saw not a human creature, nor any trace of one. We admired the variety of foliage, much of which was new to us, all in the hues of spring, and the graceful windings of the river.

∞

Mary Austin Holley, *Texas, Observations: Historical, Geographical and Descriptive in a Series of Letters* (1831)

The bay on one side—the meandering San
Jacinto or sacred hyacinth on another the back of it prairie
and timber standing in bodies and clusters like small islands
of green upon the broad waste of ocean . . . get a pilot and
sail up this beautiful stream ten miles where we enter the
mouth of Buffalo bayou . . .

∞

"J. C. Clopper's Journal and Book of Memoranda for 1828,
Province of Texas"

. . . this is the most remarkable stream I have ever seen . . . the water being of navigable depth close up to each bank giving to this most enchanting little stream the appearance of an artificial canal in the design and course of which Nature has lent her masterly hand; for its meanderings and beautiful curvatures seem to have been directed by a taste far too exquisite for human attainment—most of its course is bound in by timber and flowering shrubbery which overhang its grassy banks and dip and reflect their variegated hues in its unruffled waters . . .

∞

"J. C. Clopper's Journal and Book of Memoranda for 1828, Province of Texas"

Houston was reached late Saturday evening, after swimming the team over Buffalo bayou . . . No bridge nor ferry-boat then. There was a little flat boat that carried over a single horse or empty wagon . . . A large round tent, resembling the enclosure of a circus, was used for a drinking saloon. Plenty of "John Barley Corn" and cigars. This was the last Sunday in March, and after changing the garb of the wagoner for one similar to that worn in the city, I went out in search of a place to preach. Upon inquiry I was informed that there had never been a sermon preached in the place . . .

Monday morning ammunition was sought for in every store. Purchased two kegs of powder. No lead to be had. Family supplies and some additional articles for the soldiers were procured, and as rapidly as an ox-team, heavily loaded, could carry us, we made our way towards home.

∞

Z. N. Morrell, *Flowers and Fruits from the Wilderness* (1837)

ALONG
FORGOTTEN RIVER

Photographs of Buffalo Bayou and the Houston Ship Channel, 1997–2001

With Accounts of Early Travelers to Texas, 1767–1858

GEOFF WINNINGHAM

Texas State Historical Association

Austin

LIBRARY OF CONGRESS CATALOGING-IN-PUBLICATION DATA

Winningham, Geoff.
    Along forgotten river : photographs of Buffalo Bayou and the Houston
Ship Channel, 1997–2001 : with accounts of early travelers to Texas,
1767–1858 / by Geoff Winningham.
        p. cm.
Includes bibliographical references.
    ISBN 0-87611-189-4 — ISBN 0-87611-190-8 (limited ed.)
    1. Buffalo Bayou (Tex.)—Pictorial works. 2. Houston Ship Channel
(Tex.)—Pictorial works. 3. Houston Region (Tex.)—Pictorial works. 4.
Buffalo Bayou (Tex.)—Description and travel. 5. Houston Ship Channel
(Tex.)—Description and travel. 6. Houston Region (Tex.)—Description
and travel. I. Title.

    F394.H86 B84 2003
    917.64'14104—dc21

                                        2002153956

Published by the Texas State Historical Association in cooperation with the
Center for Studies in Texas History at the University of Texas at Austin.

The publication of this book is supported by a grant from the Wortham
Foundation, Inc.

All photographs reproduced in this book were taken by Geoff Winningham,
following the course of Buffalo Bayou and the Houston Ship Channel
through Waller, Fort Bend, Harris, Chambers, and Galveston Counties. The
accompanying accounts of early travelers to Texas refer, in most cases, to the
same region. Some of the accounts, however, describe travelers' experiences
in areas of Texas beyond these present-day counties.

page 1:   Buffalo Bayou, Cane Island Branch, Waller County
page 3:   Buffalo Bayou, Cane Island Branch, Harris County
page 5:   Marshlands along Galveston Bay, Galveston County
page 7:   Buffalo Bayou, west of Sabine Street
page 8:   Along Buffalo Bayou, downtown Houston
page 10: Behind the former Albert Thomas Convention Center,
            downtown Houston

Book design by David Timmons

Along Forgotten River

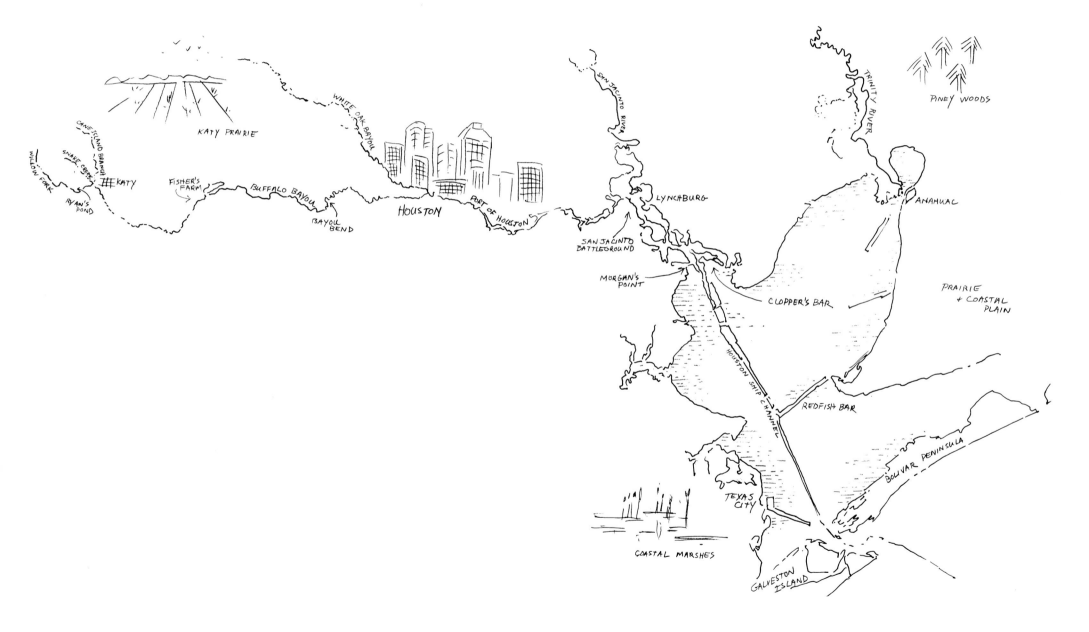

INTRODUCTION

On Christmas day, 1827, Nicholas Clopper's tiny schooner, the *Little Zoe,* came to anchor in the Gulf of Mexico off Galveston Island. It was the end of a long journey for Clopper and his three sons. From their home in Cincinnati they had traveled, first by steamer down the Ohio and Mississippi Rivers, then across the gulf from New Orleans. Beyond the sheer adventure of their voyage, the men had come to inspect the land that Clopper had purchased for his family in the province of Texas.

One of Clopper's sons, Joseph, recorded in his journal that in crossing the gulf they had left a "fiery stream" in the deep indigo waters behind their little ship, stirring up "myriads of animacula that glowed in her wake." The seas were "fearfully tumultuous," and the winds were fierce as the men approached land. One passenger's hat and Bible were torn away by the wind as he fastened himself to the ropes. Great flocks of geese and ducks flew from the shore over their vessel.

Finally, the seas calmed, the wind subsided, and all aboard felt a "return of appetite . . . freshness in the breeze" after their long journey. There was great anticipation about what lay ahead of them as they prepared to enter the treacherous waters of what is now known as Galveston Bay.

Nothing, however, had prepared them for either the beauty or the challenges of the land that they would soon encounter. Like others who would follow him in the years ahead, Clopper attempted to describe the unforgettable beauty of the wild, unspoiled land that he found. He saw enormous forests of evergreens and hardwood trees, vast prairies of waving grass—grass of such height and such enormous expanse that travelers could wander in circles for days and even perish—and canebrakes with cane stalks growing to twenty-five feet or more, "rising so high as to shut out the view of the sky as well as every terrestrial object." There were vast fields of wildflowers in the great prairies lying along the coastal plain. Crisscrossed by numerous rivers and bayous, they provided a refuge for wildlife of all kinds and included a magnificent variety of native trees, flowering shrubbery, and luxuriant undergrowth.

Some of the early travelers simply passed through the territory, while others, like Clopper, settled and made their homes here. They were a diverse lot—friars, soldiers, mapmakers, itinerant preachers, aristocratic Englishwomen, land speculators, revolutionaries, refugees, and plain farmers, the wanted and the unwanted, the privileged and the poor. Some produced written records of their travels—journals, letters home, books—writings as diverse in form and content as the travelers themselves. What they shared, however, was a desire for adventure or profit—often both—and a lasting impression of the landscape they found.

What impressed Clopper most deeply of all the natural elements of the coastal region was the stream we now know as Buffalo Bayou. In his journal he wrote that "the ebbing and flowing of the tide . . . [give] to this most enchanting little stream the appearance of an artificial canal in the design and course of which Nature has lent her masterly hand; . . . most of its course is bound in by timber and flowering shrubbery which overhang its grassy banks and dip and reflect their variegated hues in its unruffled waters." Though some traces of this luxuriant landscape survive along remote stretches of Buffalo Bayou, it is difficult for us to imagine today the pristine, magnificent beauty that Clopper and other early travelers found. By all accounts, the bayou and surrounding landscape were once a natural paradise.

Most Houstonians are aware that Buffalo Bayou was crucial in the founding and early development of our city, but few have taken more than a passing glance at the stream as it winds its way through the city. What most of us do know is that the eastern end of the bayou, on its last stretch toward Galveston Bay and the Gulf of Mexico, dredged and widened, forms the Houston Ship Channel, which has proved to be perhaps the most important single factor in the history of the city's economic growth.

Even as Clopper and his sons rafted the bayou in 1827 and 1828, changes were underway that would begin to destroy its natural beauty. Early settlers had begun to push back the native vegetation to make room for gardens and fields. Through the years, as homes and businesses were established on the banks of the bayou, the dense foliage adjacent to the water was cleared. Today, because most of the adjacent land is privately owned, it is difficult even to approach the bayou itself, except below city bridges or at a few locations at which the city has established parks. It is hardly surprising that Buffalo Bayou is virtually unknown to many Houstonians today. The only reminders that most of us have are in split-second flashes, as we dash about on the downtown overpasses of our freeways. Occasionally, as we look for our exit or change lanes, we glimpse the brown swirling waters below us or the dense foliage along the banks. Those who work on the top floors of a few of the city's skyscrapers have an entirely different impression. From their bird's-eye view they can see what Clopper called the bayou's "beautiful curvatures," its long, meandering, elegant line—"too exquisite for human attainment"—as it winds through the city on its way to the gulf.

Jan Morris, the eminent Welsh historian and essayist, came to Houston in 1980, at work on a book of essays about the great cities of the world. She did what few Houstonians do: she found her way to the banks of the bayou itself, down under the bridge at Main Street, at Allen's Landing, where the city's founders first stepped aground. In her essay on Houston, entitled "City of Destiny" and published a year later in *Texas Monthly*, Morris evoked both the mood of the bayou and a sense of its historical importance:

> . . . half hidden down there by its gloomy foliage, tentacled trees, and impenetrable brambles, there in the womb of the city slowly swirls the old brown bayou. A ponderous kind of dragonfly frequents this ancient hollow, dandelion fluff floats about, and when the water momentarily eddies, with a gas bubble perhaps or a Houston toad, really it might almost be the surfacing of one of those Texas alligators that, in prints of the first steamboat's arrival at this shore, the crew are shown shooting right and left at as they churn their passage into history.

As stirred as she was by the "old brown bayou," the other end of it, the Houston Ship Channel, impressed Morris at least as much. A century and a half after the Cloppers had made their way up the same stretch of water by raft, astonished by the natural beauty they had found there, Morris sat on the banks of the ship channel:

I went and sat upon a grassy bank beside the Houston Ship Channel, with my back to the old battleship *Texas,* the last of all the world's dreadnoughts, now berthed forever in its dock at San Jacinto State Park, and my front to the waterway itself. It is not at all a straightforward waterway, like the Suez Canal, say, since it is really only the same old Buffalo Bayou in disguise, and it winds its way sinuously up from the sea . . . gouged way at the edges by mooring berths. But up and down it night and day the sea traffic of Houston inexorably proceeds, and I sat in the sunshine there and watched it pass: tankers from Arabia, peculiar Japanese container ships, long strings of blackened barges, queer truncated tugs, oil boats of futuristic silhouette, ferries, speedboats sometimes, heavy old freighters . . . ships from the whole bloody world heading up the old bayou for Houston. And the minute they pass the battleship there, with a formal toot of their sirens sometimes, they enter a stupendous kind of ceremonial avenue, Houston's truest mall or Champs Elysées . . . for all up the banks on either side, jagged and interminable, stand the oil, chemical, and steel plants that have brought Houston into its future.

From the time I first photographed Buffalo Bayou, over twenty years ago, I wondered where and how the stream began. Did it come bubbling out of the prairie, as a primordial spring, or was it formed by the gradual confluence of numerous little creeks and tributaries? Some had suggested to me that the bayou had no real source beyond Addick's Dam, that there was nothing to be seen there except puddles of water collecting in the low spots of rice fields and prairies. I had to find out for myself, so I began to explore the western suburbs of Houston, following the bayou as best I could by car and by foot.

I first thought I had found the source of Buffalo Bayou about a mile south of the town of Katy. John Fisher, who grew up on a dairy farm along Buffalo Bayou twenty miles west of downtown, gave me a clue. I found Fisher in the process of tearing down all the old buildings on the farm. He had already moved most of the livestock off the property. All that remained was a pair of longhorn cattle, several old burros, and a miniature pony. The farm was now surrounded by huge, two-story tract homes under construction. I had stumbled upon Fisher's farm in the last days before it would disappear, its vast pastures and wooded fields soon to be the site of hundreds of new suburban homes.

"Go west on I-10 all the way to Pin Oak Road," Fisher advised me, "then go left, and you'll find the bayou—what there is of it out there—goin' under the road about a half a mile down. I think that's about as far as Buffalo Bayou goes. It must start round there somewhere."

Half an hour later, following Fisher's directions, I was thirty miles west of downtown, looking at not much more than a wide ditch, ten or fifteen feet deep, running under FM 1463. Just west of there, I could see that the bayou entered a heavily wooded area behind a small subdivision. It was impossible to tell where it went from there. I stopped a young man walking along the road and asked him if he knew where the bayou started, was it back in those trees? "I don't know," he admitted, "but Ryan, Ryan Cook, he lives over there, he knows. He's been out to that lake with all the alligators."

It took me a week to find Ryan Cook. When I did, he volunteered to take me to the lake where the bayou, so far as he knew, started. On a cold day in January, we hiked the mile or so from the highway to the lake. According to Ryan, the tiny lake has no name, and it doesn't appear on any maps that I've found. So I have named it Ryan's Pond.

"There's alligators back there. I'm sure of it," Ryan told me, pointing toward the western side of the pond. "One time a cow come outa there with his innards ripped out. The gators had got him when he come too close to the lake. He died and you can still see his bones by the lake."

The bones of cattle do indeed lie along the little pond, and whenever I ventured through the waist-high grass, sloshing through the marshy fields that lead to the lake, I did so with great apprehension. Once I heard several quick splashes ahead of me in the lake as I approached. When I reached the water, I saw what I thought at first were half a dozen baby alligators swimming just under the surface. Eventually I learned that what I had stumbled upon were "mud puppies," or "water puppies," amphibious salamanders native to the area.

I have never tired of returning to Ryan's Pond, not only because I always find new photographs to take there, but because the wildlife offers one surprise after another. I never encountered the alligators Ryan had warned me about, but that summer there were snakes everywhere, mostly water moccasins, and one afternoon I came upon a

family of wild pigs. It was a hot afternoon, and they were cooling themselves in the lake. Papa and mama pig, along with four youngsters, were almost totally submerged at the edge of the lake, with only their snouts poking out of the water. Grunting and snorting, they jumped out of the water and fled when they saw me coming. On another trip I was startled to find what I thought was a flock of pink flamingos roosting in the woods in the center of the lake. I later learned they were roseate spoonbills. Ryan's Pond became more than a source of good photographs for me. It was an introduction to the wildlife of the area, from mud puppies to wild pigs.

For the better part of two years I thought Ryan's Pond was the source of Buffalo Bayou, and I was convinced that only Ryan and I and few of his buddies knew about it. The pond appeared to be fed by drainage from the surrounding fields. On its northeastern corner it overflowed into a stream that cut through the prairie and headed east toward Houston. Later, in exploring the bayou closer to the city, I found two other tributaries, each of which flowed into Buffalo Bayou from the north. I discovered that one of the two, Cane Island Branch, originates north of the town of Katy and farther west than Ryan's Pond. It was there that I eventually found what is perhaps the most beautiful surviving stretch of Buffalo Bayou.

After several weekends of tromping through backyards and fields north of Katy, I traced Cane Island Branch to its source in what is now called the Katy Prairie. Just west of Pitt Road, in southern Waller County, there is a low spot, a sort of crease in the land, running between two adjacent rice fields. Rain and irrigation water collect there. When there is heavy rain, the water begins to flow to the east, under the road and into a pasture, though it is little more

than a trickle of water at that point. A hundred yards farther east, the trickle becomes a small stream. Tallow trees grow along the shallow banks, and I once found wild lilies in bloom there next to the water. Unless there has been especially heavy rain, the water is only a few inches deep at this point, but clearly this is the beginning of the most remote tributary of Buffalo Bayou.

A mile from from the start, in a secluded stretch of the Cane Island Branch that you can't see from the road, huge sycamore and poplar trees line its banks. The water there is often three to five feet deep and twelve feet across. In the springtime, bitterweed hangs over the water, its white blossoms falling into the water. Wild honeysuckle grows among the thick shrubbery beneath the trees.

Early one morning I sat alone under a tallow tree on the banks of Cane Island Branch. I was feeling rather proud of myself, for in my own slow and plodding way I had traced the bayou—mother of my city—to its source. Seventy-five years ago Nicolas Clopper had stood on the deck of the *Little Zoe,* anchored almost a hundred miles downstream from the peaceful, secluded little spot I had found that morning. It had taken true courage for Clopper and his sons to put aside their fears, cross Galveston Bay, and enter the little-known waters of the Rio Buffalo. I laughed at myself when I thought how timid my efforts had been compared with those of early travelers like Clopper. The only fear I had to face was that, a generation from now, my children might be unable to find even the slightest trace of the the natural paradise that Clopper and his sons had discovered along this nearly forgotten river.

Cane Island Branch, Waller County

Origins

The origins of the stream we know as Buffalo Bayou are found in the prairie north and west of the town of Katy, approximately thirty-five miles west of downtown Houston. Three small creeks originate at separate points, each flowing in a southeasterly direction and eventually coming together just south of Interstate 10. Each of these streams is classified on geological maps as intermittent; that is, they rise and fall, even disappear at times, according to rainfall conditions. Traced on a map, the three creeks form what looks like a three-pronged fork lying across the interstate highway and pointing northwest into the Katy Prairie.

The Katy Prairie lies in the Texas Coastal Plain and covers over a thousand square miles. It is bounded by the Brazos River on the southwest, by pine forests on the north, and by the city of Houston on the east. Historically, the Katy Prairie was a poorly drained tall-grassland whose ponds and wetlands harbored thousands of ducks and other waterfowl, in addition to large populations of alligators, bullfrogs, deer, antelope, black bear, turkey, and red wolves. Comanche and Karankawa Indians were the first humans to populate the prairie, following the bison herds that grazed the area.

Of the three tributaries that form Buffalo Bayou, the easternmost is Cane Island Branch. This stream originates approximately two miles north of Katy and flows almost due south. It winds its way through the town until it crosses under the interstate highway, where it continues to the south, clearly identifiable from the road by the line of tall oaks, fir, and pine trees that trace its route.

Snake Creek is the middle tributary. Beginning due west of Katy, it is the shortest and most intermittent of the three forks that form the bayou. Unless there has been a great deal of rain, it can be hard to locate this stream at all.

Willow Fork also originates due west of Katy. Its source, which also varies according to rainfall, can found approximately two miles west of Snake Creek. A noticeable line of foliage and small trees marks its banks as it moves south under the freeway, where it takes a turn to the west. When there has been ample rainfall, Willow Fork carries a considerable amount of water, and about three miles downstream from the point where it crosses under the freeway, it forms a pond. When water is high in the pond, it overflows on its eastern banks to form a short waterfall. From there, Willow Fork continues across the prairie, joining Snake Creek and Cane Island Branch as Buffalo Bayou.

PLOWED FIELD AND BUFFALO BAYOU TREE LINE, FORT BEND COUNTY

Cane Island Branch, Harris (left) and Waller (right) Counties

I had never been at all prepared for the indescribable beauty of a Texas Prairie at this season of the year . . . The wild flowers had greatly multiplied, so that they were often spread around us in the utmost profusion, and in wonderful variety. Some of those which are most cultivated in our northern gardens were here in full bloom and perfection, intermingled with many which I had never before seen, of different forms and colors . . . There was a phenomenon connected with this striking appearance, which I was at the time unable to account for . . . That was, the shrinking of the delicate plants a little in advance of us, before we had quite reached them. A friend who had witnessed the same thing, accounted for it by supposing that they received a shock through the long horizontal roots which connect them together.

∞

A Visit to Texas in 1831

KATY PRAIRIE, FORT BEND COUNTY

GRASSES, KATY PRAIRIE, FORT BEND COUNTY

The 28th [April, 1768] we passed through a very beautiful place, surrounded by thick woods called La Escaramuza: from here begins the Virgin Viperine, herb of many virtues, very medicinal. We passed along by the lake called El Francés, along by the lake of Caymán, and crossed a creek that is called El Atascadero because it is extremely miry. Here there are some large thick trees with big sharp thorns on them; if a horse falls on one, both horse and horseman remain nailed and fastened down. We crossed another that they call Caramanchel, very pleasant, with the kind of woods already mentioned. We came to the Trinity River, which is large and full of water and has pleasant banks; the stones in its bed are of very fine flint; it has many fish and some alligators. . . . Here I set up a very large holy cross of cedar.

∞

"Diary of a Visit of Inspection of the Texas Missions Made by
Fray Gaspar José de Solís in the Year 1767–68"

RYAN'S POND ON BUFFALO BAYOU, FORT BEND COUNTY

RYAN'S POND ON
BUFFALO BAYOU,
FORT BEND
COUNTY

We had advance notice that the road to the Brazos was bad, owing to continuous rains. This information was correct. Hardly had we left the city when the flat Houston prairie loomed up as an endless swamp. Large puddles of water followed one another and at several places a large section of land was under water. The long, yellow dry grass and the barren trees added to the drab appearance of the landscape. All of the low coastal region presents a similar picture during this time of the year. Any one seeing it during the winter only would get a wrong impression of the country. It has happened that persons who had the intention to settle in Texas became so discouraged upon seeing the sad picture of the Houston prairie during this time of the year, that they returned immediately to Galveston and left indignantly, concluding that all of Texas was like this region and that the reports of the natural beauty of the State were misrepresentations.

The wagons sank deeply into the mud, compelling the horses to pull them slowly, step by step. Often the wagons became so mired that it required the help of members of our company to push them out of a bog. We moved forward in this manner. Darkness fell and still we had not reached the end of the prairie, nor did we find a dry place to lie down. Impatient over the delay, I rode ahead for about an hour on the dim trail now barely discernible due to the darkness. Just as I was about to give up hope of finding a better camping place, I saw a fire in the distance and this revived my hopes of finding a camp, and also human beings. Soon I heard the tinkling bells of grazing oxen and upon riding up a small incline, I found a group of men camping under the trees near a big fire. Several prairie schooners, shaped like boats, stood nearby. The men were American farmers from the Colorado, who were bringing corn to Houston. After exchanging greetings, they invited me to stay. I unsaddled my horse and sat near them by the well-kept fire. They had eaten their supper but gave a negro boy orders to fry some bacon for me and to bake a few sweet potatoes (*Convolvulus batatas L*) in the ashes. This order was carried out in short time. Since cornbread was left over and the tin coffee can, standing by the fire, contained plenty of coffee, I had an excellent meal.

After supper I spread out my woolen saddle-blanket before the fire and chatted with my new acquaintances. They informed me that this was Pitney Point, only nine miles distant from Houston, which was often used as the first stopping place by wagons traveling between Houston and San Felipe on the Brazos.

∞

Ferdinand Roemer, *Texas, with Particular Reference to German Immigration and the Physical Appearance of the Country* (1845–47)

SOUTH KATY TO SHEPHERD DRIVE

According to the *Oxford English Dictionary, bayou* is a name given to "the marshy off-shoots and over-flowings of lakes and rivers." The roots of the word are traced to the Choctaw *bayuk*. Webster says a bayou is "a large stream or creek, or a small river, character-ized by a slow or imperceptible current." Elmer B. Atwood in *The Regional Vocabulary of Texas* distinguishes between a *creek*—a stream, smaller than a river, which usually has water in it—and a *bayou,* which he defines as "a slow-moving and . . . almost stagnant body of water." Based on these definitions, it could be said that Buffalo Bayou begins as three creeks, becomes a bayou, and ends as a river. The bayou portion of the run is from just south of the town of Katy, through western Harris County and the suburbs of Houston, up to the edge of the city itself.

South Katy, a mile or so below Interstate 10, consists primarily of the subdivisions Pin Oak Village and Falcon Point, plus a large number of widely spaced homes. It feels more like the country than the suburbs. As Buffalo Bayou flows almost due south through this community, it changes noticeably but remains within the various definitions of a bayou. At times it resembles a wide marsh, with stagnant or slow-moving water amid thick foliage and underbrush. At other points it is over twenty feet deep, lined by trees, tall grasses, and flowering shrubs, with a shallow stream trick-ling along its sandy bottom.

Searching for Buffalo Bayou farther east, along the major roads that carry traffic south of Interstate 10—Grand Parkway, Mason Road, and Fry Road—one passes through an almost endless expanse of new suburban developments.

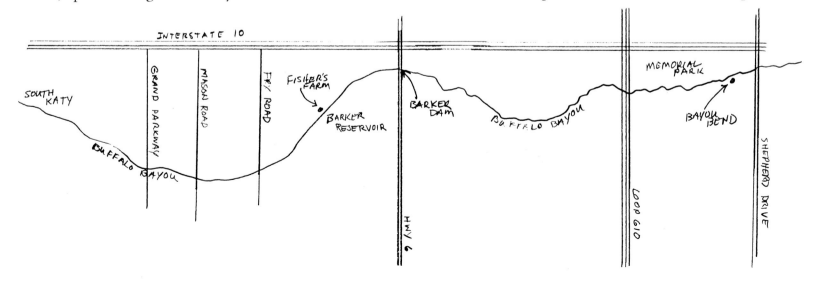

BUFFALO BAYOU, SOUTH KATY, FORT BEND COUNTY

Grand Lakes, Kelliwood Gardens, Lakeforest, and Highland Trails are but a few of the enclaves of new homes lining these thoroughfares. It is possible that none of the residents of this area know that the rather unsightly and unnamed stream crossing under each of these major streets is in fact Buffalo Bayou. "Buffalo Bayou," they will tell you, "is way over there to the east, in the reservoir, where you'll see people fishing."

Stripped of all trees and other vegetation for a hundred feet on each side of its banks, the bayou slinks anonymously through Cinco Ranch and Grand Lakes as a drainage ditch. The rare human being who parks his car by the road and makes his way down to the water may find a turtle on the banks or a nest of egrets under the bridge. But nowhere is there a sign that this is Buffalo Bayou.

Leaving the far western suburbs, the bayou turns to the northeast, crossing the Barker Reservoir, a stretch of approximately five miles. It was on the northwestern corner of the reservoir that the Fisher family's dairy farm was located, its spacious pasture and woodlands encroached upon in its final days by the ever-expanding homes of the Windsor Park Lakes subdivision. At the eastern side of the reservoir the bayou reaches Barker's Dam and Highway 6. Passing through the dam, the waters of Buffalo Bayou flow under Highway 6 and enter the near western suburbs of Houston.

The line of the bayou as it flows to the east—through the villages of Bunker Hill, Piney Point, and Hunters Creek—is increasingly sinuous. Foliage along the sandy banks becomes denser. Tall sycamores and willows overhang the water. Turtles and snakes sun themselves on overhanging limbs. Egrets roost high overhead, and alligator gar cruise just beneath the surface of the water. Some of Houston's most elegant homes are just beyond the dense trees

and brush that line the water's edge, but from a canoe, passing silently along the brown waters, civilization could not seem farther away. This stretch of Buffalo Bayou, roughly from Piney Point to Shepherd Drive, most closely resembles the natural bayou as the earliest travelers found it. How it was saved from the ambitions of real estate developers and the U.S. Army Corps of Engineers is an interesting story.

Buffalo Bayou would have been stripped of trees, straightened wherever possible, and concreted—"channelized" is the term that the Corps uses for this process—had it not been for the determined efforts of a few Houstonians over thirty years ago. Devastating floods, especially those in 1929 and 1936, had caused huge losses of property for Houstonians. In the decades that followed, the Corps of Engineers was brought in to devise means to control future flooding. The Corps' long-term plans for flood control eventually called for building the Addicks and Barker Reservoirs west of town and channelizing all the bayous.

In 1967 Terry Hershey had just moved to Houston and settled into her home off Memorial Drive, close to the banks of Buffalo Bayou. When county workers began to implement the Corps' plan to strip and straighten Buffalo Bayou, some of her neighbors got wind of it. Hershey recalls today that she and two of her friends, having heard that workers were cutting down huge trees near Chimney Rock, went to see for themselves. Astonished and saddened by what they witnessed, she called county commissioner "Squatty" Lyons the next morning, asking for an explanation. Why were work crews cutting down all the trees along Buffalo Bayou? she asked.

Thirty-four years later, she remembers Lyons' reply to her: "Mrs. Hershey, it's them big government fellas pushing

Buffalo Bayou, South Katy, Fort Bend County

us little people around." Why then, she asked, did all the trucks have Harris County written on them? "I can't talk to you now," he answered and hung up the phone. "It made me mad," Hershey says, "and I've stayed mad for thirty years. Which is a good thing, because once the Corps gets it in their heads that something should be done, it seems that no amount of reason will change their mind, no matter how bad the idea. Common sense tells you they had a bad plan, but no one wanted to talk about it."

A few months later, Terry Hershey traveled to Washington, D.C., to appear with Congressman George Bush before a House committee. After showing photographs of the concreted channels of Brays and White Oak Bayous to committee members, Bush and Hershey pleaded with them to abandon the same plan for Buffalo Bayou. The committee was persuaded, withdrew funding for the project, and Buffalo Bayou as we know it was saved, at least for the time being.

Shortly after passing under the footbridge at Bayou Bend, the former residence of Miss Ima Hogg, Buffalo Bayou approaches Shepherd Drive and Allen Parkway. The most pristine stretch of the bayou has been covered, but what lies ahead, from Shepherd to Allen's Landing, is both physically beautiful and alive with human activity.

Buffalo Bayou, Barker Reservoir, Harris County

Buffalo Bayou, Barker Reservoir, Harris County

13th . . . we came to travel through a low dirty stinking bottom   and not one solitary house log rail or board tree could we find   the most of it small ash bushes such as we use in Monroe for hand sticks   all subject to overflow from 1 to 20 ft   the land rich and stiff   The [Trinity] river a little narrow deep stinking affair   Scarcely worthy the name of river that will never be navigated with anything but a keel or flat boat on the east bank the river makes a beautiful bluff called originally Godards bluff he being the locator of the land   at this point a town has been laid off on an extensive scale called buffalo in which is one roguery one dogery & blacksmith shop combined   the keeper of the last named concern is also ferryman and is a beautiful specimen of a Texas blackguard they also have a Tavern where it was our misfortune to have to stop for two days and nights in consequence of Terrys sickness   the keeper of the concern is a big buffalo looking fellow who came from Tennessee to Arkansas he keeps about him a crowd of the filthiest looking loafers we have ever seen any where in this whole country of loafers . . .

. . . In this portion of the country we were much perplexed to obtain supplies of any kind for either love or money particularly bread   in our extremeity T C M went to one house and asked for bread   the reply was we have no meal or no flour neither   he then asked for meat   the reply was we have no bacon nor no buffalo meat neither   he then asked them if they had anything that would do for food for our horses   they told him they had no corn no fodder no oats neither   Said he Sir how do you do   then his reply was tolerable well thank you how do you do yourself

At an other we asked the same questions and when I come to corn they asked us if we had a waggon   we told them no   their answer was V. well   if you dont want none for your waggons I spect we could spare you the matter of one or two tins full for your horses. We left him thinking beware young man the fool killer might come around before you expect him . . .

16th Terry some better   started early   rode 10 miles through country pretty well divided between timber and praira [sic] the timber Post-oak with some hickory occasionally some black Jack Some of the soil stiff and some sandy   none verry rich until we got out 10 miles then a shade better . . . we traveled 3 miles farther through a Praira . . . at this place (Weirs) we found spring water as they call it we call It Puddle water and verry mean Puddle water at that. . . .

17th . . . Terry seemed much better and from his motions seemed to be more himself again. In the evening from Reevs to Brutons 8 miles along a dim path and strange to say without getting lost through a flat sandy Post oak country generally poor   no water but the meanest sort of puddle water. . . . Corn here seems to grow like the timber rather scrubby, as to the ear it bears we know nothing, as we have seen too few of the article to form a correct judgment. Brutons wife we found sick therefore we conclude the country is sickley   If this circumstance is not conclusive, the general appearance of the country and the scarcity of good water makes the thing in our estimation conclusive   To night Terry had a good sweat   rose early eat hearty and reported himself ready for shirt tail popping in the direction of home . . .

∞

A. W. Moore, "A Reconnoissance in Texas in 1846"

On the 22nd [April, 1768] we crossed the creek of La Soledad, much foliage and covered with many trees which I have mentioned above. We crossed another that is called Juana Rosa, as pleasant as the foregoing. These creeks are the habitat of the Cocos, a little farther on than the last in a little glade, the road turns aside to the right for the Presidio and Mission of Orcoquisac. Afterwards we passed through La Mota del India, and came to a stop at the Bernavé creek. It has good water and the road leads through very pleasant woods, through plains and green and flowery hills abundant in deer, turkeys, quail, buffalo, bear, and many Spanish cattle, unbranded and without owner, because the first person who entered when these lands were discovered and conquered, was Captain Leon (of glorious memory). On the bank of these rivers he left a bull and a cow, a horse and a mare, and this is the reason why there are so many cattle and horses unbranded and wild.

∞

"Diary of a Visit of Inspection of the Texas Missions Made by
Fray Gaspar José de Solís in the Year 1767–68"

MEADOW AND BUFFALO BAYOU TREE LINE, FISHER'S FARM, HARRIS COUNTY

Buffalo Bayou, Terry Hershey Park, west Houston

December 28, 1833.—*Moving from Harrisburg, continued.*

It was anything but fun before we got to the end of our journey. Three miles from town we left the timber. The prairie was covered with water. Bray's Bayou had overflowed and the road looked like a river. We hadn't traveled six miles when the sun set, and the party on horseback was not in sight. We came to a mound that was high and dry, and Mr. Lytle said we would camp. He hobbled the oxen and turned them loose so they could feed. He got pine knots to make a fire . . .

The men came back. Father had killed a deer. He soon made a fire, and the young men went to the timber to get firewood. They had to stand in the water, cut down a tree, cut it up, tie it on their saddles, and walk back. While the men were gone, father skinned the deer and got it ready for cooking.

We were waiting for the wood men to return, when all of a sudden the wolves began howling. They surrounded the camp. Mr. Lytle drove the oxen back, and tied them to the cart. The wolves were after the venison. Father would have shot one, but said if he killed it the others would eat it and then kill the oxen. Our wood-men got back, and made a big fire, which scared the wolves. They ran a short distance, sat down, faced the cart, and barked and howled all night. The men had to hold their horses to keep them from running off. One of the men had a mare and a colt. He couldn't catch the colt; it would kick at the men, run off, and back to its mother. Father had two hound dogs for hunting. They hid under the cart, and one of the men advised father to kill the dogs and feed the wolves. Mother, sister, and I, slept in the cart, brother and the dogs underneath. The men sat up to guard the stock. Bray's Bayou was near. We were surrounded by wolves and water. There was a large sycamore tree that stood in the water near us, and it was as white as snow. The buzzards roosted in it. We could hear owls hoot all night. Mother said it was a night of horrors . . . She said the owls were singing a funeral dirge, and the wolves and buzzards were waiting to bury us. At daylight the wolves and owls disappeared.

∞

"The Reminiscences of Mrs. Dilue Harris"

BUFFALO BAYOU, TERRY HERSHEY PARK, WEST HOUSTON

In the fall of 1858 a couple of ships, presumably British, anchored at Galveston under suspicious circumstances. They were first thought to be slavers watching for an opportunity of secretly landing their human freight. But the ships turned out to be laden only with camels; at least no evidence appeared that they had any African negroes aboard to sell as slaves. Happening to be in Galveston at the time, I went to see the camels (about forty in number), after they had been landed and penned. Mrs. Watson, an English lady, owner of the herd, was hunting some reliable person to whom she might intrust its care till finally disposed of by sale or otherwise. I was introduced as a proper person to the lady, and her agent, Senor Michado. A few preliminaries once settled as to the extent of my obligations for their safety, I contracted with Senor Michado on satisfactory terms to assume the custody and maintenance of the camels when delivered at my ranch. Accordingly a steamboat was chartered, on which Michado brought the animals to the mouth of Sims' Bayou for delivery. The landing took place in the presence of a crowd of spectators, among whom were Sam Allen, Jules Baron (my brother-in-law), and myself. On finding themselves more once on solid ground, they showed their high spirits by jumping, rearing, and frisking about like sheep. Observing these capers, Baron remarked that he did not believe that anyone could lasso a camel. Allen quickly affirmed the contrary, and finally bet Baron $10 that he could rope one himself. Allen mounted his horse, lasso in hand, and, with a sharp swing, on the first trial threw it over the head of a large camel and brought him to the ground after a short struggle. Baron, lately in from Louisiana, had not learned that Texans generally accomplish what they undertake. Michado, with his outlandish servants, Turks or Arabs of unpronounceable names, conducted the camels to my ranch, a few miles distant. Here they were easily corraled in the pasture prepared for them . . .

The camels were naturally a great curiosity for Texans, and our neighbors, and people from a distance, flocked in to see the strange sight. The camels were quite obedient to their Arab keepers, kneeling and rising at word of command. In going to Houston, six miles distant, the Arabs would ride a camel each, and their entry and exit would always create a sensation among the people in town seeing them for the first time.

∞

Francis Richard Lubbock, *Six Decades in Texas*

Buffalo Bayou, River Oaks area

HOUSTON, JULY 23RD, 1850

Miss Ellen A. Taylor, Charleston, S.C.
From Horace D. Taylor
My Dear Sister Ellen:

. . . *If you was here* I would take you to ride
every evening either Horseback or in a carriage. I have just
got down from the Country a Horse which I raised and he
is not only very handsome but he is a fine Buggy horse
and fairly makes a carriage spin. I had a terrible time with
him a few days since. He was turned loose in the pasture
and immediately started for the Bayou which partly sur-
rounds the ground, and he plunged in and swam to the
opposite shore. It being very boggy he could not get out
and was soon entangled in vines. The prospects were very
fair for his drowning, so I plunged in and broke the vines
which held him. He then succeeded in reaching shore
again and finally got on solid ground nearly exhausted. We
both presented a sad appearance when safe out of the
scrape. I believe I got the worst of it as I was considerably
bruised and my face and hands badly scratched by briers—
so much that I was almost ashamed to appear in company
where there were Ladies, but my wounds passed as honor-
able once I related to them the incidents connected with
their appearance. Although some pretended to believe I
had had a cat fight. . . .

Your affec[tionate] Bro
Horace D. Taylor

∞

Early Days on the Bayou, 1838–1890: The Life and Letters of
Horace Dickinson Taylor

Buffalo Bayou, Memorial Park area

A dozen of us rode to the mouth of the Brazos to pass the day & get fish and oysters. One of the party, with Lucifer, set fire to the prairie & produced the finest scene I ever witnessed or imagined. There was some wind, & with us. The fire spread at such a rate we had to whip up our horses, & the last of the party [had] to ride through the line of fire. We left it far behind & could see it burning briskly all day. Returning as the sun was setting brilliantly behind us—the roaring sea at our right—nothing but a sheet of fire before—The company paired off galloping in divergent lines, from Mr. Somerville & myself in the rear. The curlews were singing—the cranes screaming—the deer & cattle scampering. Never was anything so beautiful. Think of a prairie large as a sea with all these objects spread out wide—grass, without a track under our feet. We approached the line of flame extending to the right & left 8 or 10 miles—We approached & saw our whole company pass within. Though it seems a line, there are frequent spaces of many yards where you can pass—the heat of grass is not great. In this pass the smoke & flame curled up high like an arch. I said to my companion that looks like the door of a nameless place—"yes," he said, "& if we don't make haste we shall not enter." True, it was closed before we reached it, our company on the other side, & we had to seek another. When we were within, the ground being all burnt over, it was as black as Erebus. There was another line of fire far ahead & to the right & left—a complete picture of the fanatic's Hell, except there were no yawning monsters, except those of the imagination. I felt no terrors but those of being lost, for the darkness was made visible by the distant, lurid lights—like burning cities. The scene was strange & grand. As the idea was creeping over me of being kept out all night (as often happens on those prairies, from the sameness of the scenery at night) a welcome halloo from those ahead reassured my spirits. As we passed the outer confines of this Hades (reaching the space the fire had been all day running over at the speed of a race horse) the moon rose in splendor—& the stars around her glistened. Never did I experience so much of the true sublime.

∞

Letters of an Early American Traveller, Mary Austin Holley: Her Life and Her Works, 1784–1846

ALLEN PARKWAY TO CENTRAL HOUSTON

With huge oaks, towering sycamore trees, and lush willows overhanging its banks, the bayou makes its approach to the city's center through a winding corridor along Allen Parkway. Jogging and biking paths wind through the trees and along the banks of the bayou. The beauty and charm of the natural landscape along Buffalo Bayou at Allen Parkway attract hundreds, even thousands, of runners, bikers, and nature lovers during afternoon hours and weekends.

In the summer months, from the bridges at Waugh Drive and Studemont Street, those who stop and look carefully down into the brown waters can often see an alligator gar, two or three feet long, patrolling the waters like a slow-moving torpedo. Dragonflies buzz about. Pampas grass and cane stand up to fifteen feet high in patches along the banks. Joggers who use the trails here will tell you about seeing an occasional alligator lurking in the water. The big trees, lush vegetation, and wildlife are in stark contrast to other bayous in the city, notably Brays and White Oak, which have been stripped of virtually all vegetation, straightened, and then paved with concrete.

In 1949, almost twenty years before Terry Hershey and George Bush saved the stretch of Buffalo Bayou along Memorial Park, this stretch of the bayou was stripped of trees, cleared, and regraded by the Army Corps of Engineers. Citizens' protests and newspaper editorials might have had some effect in stopping them short of concreting the bayou's banks. For whatever reason, it didn't happen, and today, over fifty years later, this stretch of Buffalo Bayou has made a grand recovery. Native trees planted decades ago now tower over the water. Some will point out that this is not Buffalo Bayou as it was in its original state, that we have destroyed that forever. Yet this is surely one of the most beautiful and most utilized green spaces in the city, and the elegant, meandering line of the bayou is still there, leading us into the heart of Houston.

Approaching the city by canoe, just east of the

64

Buffalo Bayou along Allen Parkway

Studemont Street bridge, skyscrapers seem to rise suddenly out of the water. They hang above the water like apparitions, shimmering for an instant on the surface. Then they disappear as the bayou takes another turn, weaving its way in serpentine curves toward the heart of the city.

At the end of Allen Parkway, the waters flow under the Sabine Street bridge. Buffalo Bayou has become a true river at this point, with a depth of at least ten feet, even in dry seasons, and a width of thirty to thirty-five feet.

At almost any hour of the day, a few people can be found fishing or sleeping on the bayou's sandy banks. Some are what we would call the homeless; others simply seem to be content here with the turtles, the dragonflies, and an occasional egret. The incessant hum of city traffic drifts down from freeways high overhead. Debris carried downstream after the most recent rains is lodged overhead in branches and bridge pilings. What trees and vegetation have survived seem to be in need of a breath of fresh air and sunshine. For many years, this stretch of the bayou was a shadowy, murky, ominous place, even during daylight hours. Any soul brave enough to venture down here at night might have been reminded of the River Styx, except for the tall, glistening buildings of downtown, reflecting off the surface of the dark waters.

The landscape along the bayou downtown has been changing rapidly in recent years. Architects and landscape designers have been hard at work, making this a more inviting place for the general public. Possibly San Antonio's Riverwalk has inspired them to develop this stretch of the bayou. Allen's Landing, where the city fathers stepped ashore to found the city over a century and a half ago, is getting a facelift. There are spotless new benches and handsome signs noting the historic importance of the spot. More than a few fine old trees were lost, though, where bulldozers cleared the land for a parking lot.

THE BAYOU ALONG ALLEN PARKWAY

ALONG ALLEN PARKWAY

ALONG BUFFALO BAYOU
AND ALLEN PARKWAY

While wandering about, we were entertained by a spectacle, the like of which surpassed anything in vividness I remember seeing in Texas. Glowworms flew over the long grass of the prairie in such countless numbers and emitted such bright rays of light that the eye was actually blinded or dazzled and one imagined one's self to be in the midst of a rain of fire.

∞

Ferdinand Roemer, *Texas, with Particular Reference to German Immigration and the Physical Appearance of the Country* (1845–47)

Along Allen Parkway near downtown

ALONG BUFFALO BAYOU AND ALLEN PARKWAY

The day before we left San Antonio

was cold and foggy. The following morning was warm but still foggy, making our ride, with a light wind behind us, exceedingly oppressive. We threw off our coats, and soon stripped off vest and cravat; but this, we found, was not enough, and we were obliged to stop to take off our flannel. Our horses were reeking with sweat. At two o'clock the thermometer, in a cool, shady spot, stood at 79°, and the sky was nearly clear. We were very tired and thirsty, and one of us suggested that this was the very country and the very weather for mirage. It was not long after we saw the edge of the horizon rising in the flickering heat, and groups of trees standing free in the air, as an island or a point stretches off into the sky of a hot day on the sea-coast. Then the trees connected themselves with the land below upon each side, and we saw a beautiful lake, the water rippling in the sunlight. It grew wider and longer, and shortly was like the open sea, with a rich and shady shore, extending up, at intervals, like bays and rivers, into the land. Soon the lakes were common here and there about us, calm of surface, trees with heavy foliage bending over their banks to rest in the water. Had we not been prepared, by a knowledge of the country, we should have been strongly tempted to ride towards some of them for a drink of cool water.

∞

Frederick Law Olmsted, *A Journey through Texas; or, a Saddle-Trip on the Southwestern Frontier* (1852–57)

Later in the day, the air became clearer, and a pleasant breeze played upon our backs. The mirage gradually disappeared, and we lost it in descending a swell of the prairie. It was near sunset, with a dull cloud bank in the north. We were still suffering with the heat, when one of us said—

"See this before us, what is it, fog again or smoke?"

"A prairie fire, I think," said the other.

"Probably it is; but what is this on the hill close by, this is fog, surely? It must be a norther coming? Yes, it is a norther; listen to that roar! We must get our clothing on or we shall be chilled through."

First, a chilly whiff, then a puff, the grass bends flat, and, bang, it is upon us—a blast that would have taken a top-gallant sail smack out of the bolt-ropes, and cold as if blowing across a sea of ice. We galloped to the nearest ravine, and hurried on all the clothing we could muster.

∞

Frederick Law Olmsted, *A Journey through Texas; or, a Saddle-Trip on the Southwestern Frontier* (1852–57)

ICE STORM, ALONG BUFFALO BAYOU, WEST OF SABINE STREET

. . . often along these shady banks have I rowed my little skiff and wondered if ever some Bard had consecrated its border shades by a correspondent flow of song—if some native Ossian had ever breathed forth in his artless strains the dictates of an inspired Muse. I thought of other streams immortalized, and thought that this might by its enchanting beauties give immortality to some future Bard—for it can not forever be "by fame neglected and unknown to song" and "creep inglorious like a vulgar stream."

∽

"J. C. Clopper's Journal and Book of Memoranda for 1828, Province of Texas"

. . . *No boat had ever been* above this place [Harrisburg], and we were three days making the distance to Houston, only six miles by the dirt road, but twelve by the bayou. The slow time was in consequence of the obstructions we were compelled to remove as we progressed. We had to rig what were called Spanish windlasses on the shore to heave the logs and snags out of our way, the passengers all working faithfully. All hands on board would get out on the shore, and cutting down a tree would make of it a windlass by boring holes in it and placing it upon a support and throwing a bight of rope around it, secure one end to a tree in the rear and the other to the snags or fallen trees in the water. Then by means of the capstan bars we would turn the improvised capstan on land, and draw from the track of our steamer the obstructions. Capitalist, dignified judge, military heroes, young merchant in fine clothes from the dressiest city in the United States, all lent a helping hand. It being necessary to lie by at night, in the evenings we had a good time dancing and frolicking with the settlers on the shore, who were delighted to see "newcomers from the States."

Just before reaching our destination a party of us, becoming weary of the steamer, took a yawl and concluded we would hunt for the city. So little evidence could we see of a landing that we passed by the site and run into White Oak Bayou, only realizing that we must have passed the city when we struck in the brush. We then backed down the bayou, and by close observation discovered a road or street laid off from the water's edge. Upon landing we found stakes and footprints, indicating that we were in the town tract.

∞

Francis Richard Lubbock, *Six Decades in Texas* (1837)

City of Houston, from Buffalo Bayou, west of downtown

This was about the first of January, 1837, when I discovered Houston. For though I did not accompany Columbus when he discovered America, as is asserted, I certainly was in at the discovery of Houston, the Laura being the first steamer that ever reached her landing. Wharves were not in Texas.

A few tents were located not far away; one large one was used as a saloon. Several small houses were in the course of erection. Logs were being hauled in from the forest for a hotel to be erected (where the Hutchins House now stands) by Col. Benjamin Fort Smith, who was the inspector-general at the battle of San Jacinto. A small number of workmen were preparing to build cabins, business houses, and this hotel. We boarded on the steamer for several days, and in the meantime hastened business upon the shore.

Immediately I made a contract with the agent of the Allens, J. S. Holman, to have put up for me a small clapboard house on a lot that I had purchased from the town company, paying $250 for the lot and $250 for the house. This was built of three-foot pine boards and covered with three-foot boards, and contained all told one room about twelve feet square and a smaller shed room. There was one door leading into the main room and one door from that room into the shed room, both of three-foot boards, with all hinges and fastenings made of wood. There was no window in the house. When air and light were wanted, a board was knocked off. A few rough boards were laid down for the floor, not extending under the bed. . . . The bedstead put up in the corner was made by driving forked sticks into the ground and laying poles across with clapboards for slats to support the moss mattress.

∞

Francis Richard Lubbock, *Six Decades in Texas*

...*When fall came* with its northers and there were only three stoves in the whole of Houston, we used to light fires in front of the saloon in the evening, stand around them and enjoy—not excepting the President— hot drinks with merry speeches. The City Hotel was then the chief gathering place. In that spacious wooden shack we were often 100 and 150 at the table. All the nations were represented. One could hear of the most interesting careers. There were frequent brawls, pistols were drawn, bowie knifes flashed, and as everyone walked about well armed, these incidents looked rather dangerous. I twice witnessed scenes where first in the barroom and afterwards in the streets, men were wounded in this manner. The police in those days tried to maintain peace and avert disaster, to be sure, but rarely happened that anyone was arrested. Games of hazard were forbidden but nevertheless the green tables were occupied by the gamblers for whole nights. What is more, these blacklegs even formed a regular guild against which any opposition was risky matter. The resident citizens, however, who were intent on the peace and good reputation of their new dwelling place, checked with all their might the nuisance that had gained ground.

There was lively and varied activity going on in Houston at that time. Steamboats from Galveston tied up daily. The owners of land certificates, who had selected the finest free land, and tradesmen of all sorts arrived on horseback from the interior of the country, among them many a Mexican smuggler. They brought news from the frontier, pointed out the beauty of newly discovered regions, and described their adventures with the Indians and wild beasts. In short, time passed quickly; being kept in a state of excitement, people forgot all their privations.

∞

Gustav Dresel's Houston Journal: Adventures in North America and Texas, 1837–1841

My first visit to Houston was in winter. It was late at night when, after a long ride from the frontier of the Indian territory, where snow was still on the ground, I

"Dropt into that magic land."

Stepping from the train, I walked beneath skies which seemed Italian. The stillness, the warmth, the delicious dreaminess, the delicate languor were most intoxicating. A faint breeze, with a hint of perfume in it, came through the lattice of my window at the hotel. The magnolias sent their welcome; the roses, the dense beds of fragrant blossoms, exhaled their greeting. Roses bloom all winter, and in the early spring and May the gardens are filled with them.

∞

Edward King, *The Great South* (1873–74)

Buffalo Bayou, under Interstate 45

Wednesday, May 10.—It rained again today, but we pushed on in the gig toward Houston. The rain had, however, so swollen the water of the bayou and increased the current that we were eight hours rowing twelve miles.

Monday, May 15.—We landed at Houston, the capital of Texas, drenched to the skin, and were kindly received on board the steamer *Yellow Stone*, Captain West, who gave us his stateroom to change our clothes in, and furnished us refreshments and dinner. The Buffalo Bayou had risen about six feet, and the neighboring prairies were partly covered with water; there was a wild and desolate look cast on the surrounding scenery. We had already passed two little girls encamped on the bank of the bayou under the cover of a few class-boards [*sic*] . . . cooking a scanty meal; shanties, cargoes of hogsheads, barrels, etc., were spread about the landing; and Indians drunk and hallooing were stumbling about in the mud in every direction. . . .

We returned to our boat through a mêlée of Indians and blackguards of all sorts. In giving a last glance back we once more noticed a number of horses rambling about the grounds, or tied beneath the few trees that have been spared by the axe. We also saw a liberty pole, erected on the anniversary of the battle of San Jacinto, on the twenty-first of last April, and were informed that a brave tar who rigged the Texan flag on that occasion had been personally rewarded by President Houston with a town lot, a doubloon, and the privilege of keeping a ferry across the Buffalo Bayou at the town, where the bayou forks diverge in opposite directions.

Tuesday, May 16.—Departed for New Washington . . .

∞

John James Audubon, Journal

DOWNTOWN HOUSTON, BUFFALO BAYOU

. . . The main street of this city of a year [Houston] extends from the landing into the prairie—a beautiful plain of some six miles wide, & extending, with points and islands of timber, quite to the Brazos. On this main street are two large hotels, 2 stories, with galleries (crowded to overflowing) several stores 2 stories—painted white—one block of eleven stores (rent $500 each)—some 2 story dwelling houses—& then the capitol—seventy feet front—140 rear—painted peach blossom about ¼ mile from the landing. Other streets, parallel, & at right angles, are built on here & there, but chiefly designated by stakes. One story buildings are scattered in the edge of the timber which forms an amphitheatre round the prairie, according to the bend of the Bayou, which, being wider, would render this a most eligible town site. As it is, it is too inconvenient, besides being unhealthy & a removal of the government is talked of.

Congress had adjourned when we arrived—remaining members called on us, with many other persons, whom we received in the cabin. We kept our lodging in the boat, at the city so comfortable. The President returned from a visit to the country next day & came immediately to pay us his respects. He afterwards dined with us 2 days one of which was Sunday, & gallanted us to the Capitol, in one wing of which is a gallery of portraits of distinguished characters of the last campaign. You see the arts flourish in this new land already.

Attended church there in the morning—Expecting to hear Dr. Ruter, who has been preaching there—was absent—heard miserable canting about turning *swords* into *pruning hooks*—premature.

∞

Letters of an Early American Traveller, Mary Austin Holley: Her Life and Her Works, 1784–1846

Downtown Houston

JUNE, 1836.—*Shipping Cotton on a Flatboat*

. . . The new town laid out by the Allens was
named Houston, in honor of General Houston. There were
circulars and drawings sent out, which represented a large
city, showing churches, a courthouse, a market house and a
square of ground set aside to use for a building for Congress, if the seat of government should be located there. . . .
There was so much excitement about the city of Houston
that some of the young men in our neighborhood, my
brother among them, visited it. After being absent some
time they said that it was hard work to find the city in the
pine woods; and that, when they did, it consisted of one
dugout canoe, a bottle gourd of whiskey and a surveyor's
chain and compass, and was inhabited by four men with an
ordinary camping outfit. We had a good joke on the boys
at their disappointment. We asked them at what hotel they
put up, and whether they went to church and to the the-
ater. They took our teasing in good part and said they were
thankful to get home alive. They said the mosquitoes were
as large as grasshoppers, and that to get away from them
they went bathing. The bayou water was clear and cool,
and they thought they would have a nice bath, but in a few
minutes the water was alive with alligators. One man ran
out on the north side, and the others, who had come out
where they went in, got a canoe and rescued him. He said
a large panther had been near by, but that it ran off as the
canoe approached . . .

∞

"The Reminiscences of Mrs. Dilue Harris"

Buffalo Bayou and downtown Houston

UNDER INTERSTATE 45, DOWNTOWN HOUSTON

At that time fifteen hundred to two thousand people, mostly men, were living together in Houston in the most dissimilar manner. The President, the whole personnel of the government, many lawyers who found ample means of support in those new regions, a large number of gamblers, tradesman, artisans, former soldiers, adventurers, curious travelers from the United States, about a hundred Mexican prisoners who made suitable servants, daily new troops of Indians—all associated like chums on an equal footing.

Crimes, the desire for adventure, unfortunate circumstances of all sorts, love of freedom, and the fair prospect of gain had formed this quaint gathering. It was everyone's wish to be somebody in the general company, and therefore everyone threw the veil of oblivion over past deeds. Everyone stood on his own merit. No family connections, former fortune, rank, or claims had any influence on present civic position. The constitution of Texas, which is purely republican and is taken from the Code Napoléon and the constitutions of Mexico, and particularly the constitution of Louisiana, grants everyone who distinguishes himself for the general welfare the opportunity to attain the highest offices of the country by means of elections. Only talent, or rather its useful application, is taken into account. Not birth nor a bold front, but the vote of the people, turns the scale.

∞

Gustav Dresel's Houston Journal: Adventures in North America and Texas, 1837–1841

At seven o'clock in the morning

we arrived at the pretty town of Houston; it is built on high land, and the banks, which are covered with evergreens, rise abruptly from the river [Buffalo Bayou]. There are plenty of inns at Houston, such as they are, and we took up our quarters at the "Houston House," a large shambling wooden building, kept by a Captain or Colonel Baldwin, one of the most civil, obliging people I ever saw. We had a sitting room which was weather proof, though to keep out the intense cold was impossible. It was said that our landlord was anxious to add to the comforts of his house, but he had a great many bad debts; it was, he told us, a losing concern altogether; more went out that came in, and only that morning, having asked a gentleman to pay his bill, the reply was, "If you come to insult me again sir, by—— I'll shoot you sir." We went down to breakfast in the public room; the food consisted of tough beef-steaks, each as large as a good sized dish, eggs hardly warmed through, and emptied over the meat, and squirrels; each guest did not remain more than five minutes, and on his retiring, his place was immediately filled by another hungry traveller. I looked on in silent wonder at their extraordinary powers of mastication; one old man in particular, in a green maize coat, outdid all the rest. I could not have believed any human being could have contrived to stow away such a cargo of "dry goods" in so short a time.

∞

Matilda Charlotte (Jesse) Fraser Houstoun, *Texas and the Gulf Coast of Mexico; or, Yachting in the New World* (1842)

UNDER THE SABINE STREET BRIDGE

Friday, January 19. Embark on the *Sam Houston* (Steam Boat) a small filthy, horribly managed concern, for Houston, seventy-five miles distant. Bot refuses to take Texas money for passage. Ground on Red Fish bar, seventeen miles distant.

Saturday, January 20. Attempting all day to get off, succeed at night. Fare distressingly bad, Crackers, potatoes, . . . Beef (tough) Coffee (very bad).

Sunday, January 21. We proceed to Clopper's bar, seventeen miles further and stick. Work all day unsuccessfully to get off. Passengers dissatisfied; some speak of going ashore and walking up forty miles but decline.

Monday, January 22. Self and . . . others go ashore hunting. I killed a fine deer running, entrusted him to the care of the boatswain who hang him up and the Buzzards eat ¾ths of it. Much prairie, but little timber. Went to several cottages and found the inmates very hospitable. Had an enjoyable dinner. The passengers much chagrined upon our report of fare &C., regret they did not go. Now they will go tomorrow. Land on the schooner *Mobile* where I found Capt. C. L. Owens of Kentucky, for whom I had letters and a bundle.

Tuesday, January 23. Get off the bar. Venison stake for Breakfast, the remnants of the buzzards' feast. All countenances brighten, good cheer all day. Pass by Lynchburg opposite the battlegrounds of San Jacinto, thence up the Buffalo Bayou by Harrisburg which was burnt by the Mexicans and on up to Houston. . . .

Wednesday, January 24. Took lodgings at Floyd's Hotel. Invited by Jackson Smith Esq. to take part of his room and bed. Do so and find it superior to anything of its kind in Texas. Rains, streets become very muddy in a few hours. Visit Billiard room, play game of Billiards, successful. In the same house are four Faro Banks in addition to which are a number of others in the place, the greatest sink of disipation and vice that modern times have known. Place but nine months old and has a population of 2000.

Thursday, January 25. Clifton Prewitt taken sick at the Statehouse. Had him brot to the house. Give him medicin. . . .

Friday, January 26. Streets still muddy. Prewitt seems a little better but has taken some Brandy which may operate unfavorably. . . . Went to Secretary of Navy's office. Met there Henry Ham, an acquaintance. Returned. Took game of Billiards, successful again. Bad fare at the hotel. . . .

Tuesday, January 30. Visiting. Several rows in town, man killed. Prewitt a little better. Cold.

Wednesday, January 31. Prewitt wors, confined by him most of day. . . .

Thursday, February 1. Prewitt much worse. Remained with him all day. Rainy.

Friday, February 2. Rain all day and night. Prewitt in Statu Quo. Self a little unwell.

Saturday, February 3. Much same.

Sunday, February 4. Despair of Prewitt's recovery, three physicians cup him. Several persons freeze to death.

Monday, February 5. Quite unwell, eat nothing. Prewitt died at 4 P.M. . . .

Tuesday, February 6. Buried him genteely at the city burying ground, one mile from city. Walked out. Very warm. Unwell in the evening.

Wednesday, February 7. Go to the country. Find it very pretty but not rich. Feel a little better. . . .

Thursday, March 22. Fine day. Four criminals whipped at the post. Steam Boats *Laura*, *Sam Houston* and *Archer* arrived *Correo* cleared. Mail arrived but brought no letters for me. Much vexed. Colonel Love got home. Jones convicted of murder, a plainer case than which has seldom been submitted to a Jury. Counsel attempt to take advantage of legal technicalities and imperfections in pleadings.

Friday, March 23. Cloudy in the morning but cleared off beautifully by noon. Colonel Wigginton left for the Brazos. Quick convicted of murder, a case similar to Jones'. Quick a savage bloodthirsty, malicious looking devil, who changed not a feature or mussel of his face upon the verdict being announced. Grand Jury discharged after having presented 270 indictments: 4 for Murder, 4 treason, 8 arson, 40 Larceny. The Bar gave a supper to the grand jury, high meeting, some gloriously drunk. Dreamed of kissing Willina &c. &c. &c. . . .

Monday, March 26. A morning in "Statu Quo." Harwood left for Washington with groceries. Took two Bowie knives for me to sell. Loaned him my rifle. Broke the chain of my watch. Called on several friends. Calls returned. Supped at Woodruff's where I had *Milk*, Corn bread and butter. Jones the convict attempted to kill himself by shooting but shot over his head. . . .

Tuesday, March 27. Morning cloudy and warm. Went out to Woodruff's to breakfast. Took a wash in well water. Counted nineteen young calves in the pen. Returned by the slaughter hous where I saw upwards of two hundred beeves' heads, a little further and I saw a pretty girl . . . Dined at Woodruff's. Saw judge Smith who invited me out to see him. Went to the ball at 9 O'clock and returned at 4, forty gentlemen and as many ladies in attendance. Had a fine set, supper, good wines and interesting ladies. Equal all in all to a Kentucky Ball. Mrs. Lively, a very pretty lady, fell flat on the floor in a dance. A gentleman also came to his marrow bones. The ladies have rather large feet, owing perhaps to their having gone barefooted a little too long.

Wednesday, March 28. A delightful day, worthy of other deeds. One hundred forty men ordered out to guard the criminals to the gallows. A concourse of from 2000 to 3000 persons on the ground and among the whole not a single sympathetic tear was dropped. Quick addressed the crowd in a stern, composed and hardened manner entirely unmoved up to the moment of swinging off the cart. Jones seemed frightened altho' as hardened in crime as Quick. They swung off at 2 Oclock P.M. and were cut down in thirty-five Minutes, not having made the slightest struggle. . . . Drs. Price and Watson, Snow, Cavanaugh and self went out to the graves and cut off the heads of Quick and Jones and brought them in for dissection. Supped at Woodruff's, good supper.

∞

John Hunter Herndon, "Diary of a Young Man in Houston, 1838"

Saturday, April 14. Warm, clear day. House convened at 10 A.M. Ladies began to assemble soon after and by 11½ the house was full, at which time the President entered in a very dignified, graceful manner and took his seat. After having sat a few moments and surveyed the audience he arose and in a clear and impressive style addressed both houses for one hour, giving satisfaction to every auditor. But the meeting was not permitted to pass off in this happy manner. As the crowd were dispersing, Ward made an attack upon Lubbock, Comptroller, who after being knocked down and arising shot at Ward without effect. Thus ended that matter for the present. Two hours afterwards Seavy and Armstrong fell out and fought. After they had been separated Seavy went out and provided himself with a pistol, returned and shot Armstrong in the back of the head from which he died immediately. Seavy is in jail and will unquestionably be hung and thus endeth this affair. I am just informed all the justices in town are now employed in the investigation of crime: One for Murder, another for Counterfeiting and others for petit larceny. What a den of villains must there not be here? . . .

∞

John Hunter Herndon, "Diary of a Young Man in Houston, 1838"

FISHING IN BUFFALO BAYOU, DOWNTOWN HOUSTON

Along Buffalo Bayou, downtown Houston

The night was truly gorgeous. The Germans have a saying that the sky seems *nearer* in Texas than in Europe. The stars, and especially the nebulae, do seem to shine more vividly, and to give more light, and the firmament appears more effulgent than in any part of the northern or southern hemisphere in which I have been. The air was nearly calm, but elastic, and of an agreeable temperature. It is difficult to express the delicious freshness of the gentle breeze that flows across your cheek, upon such an open pillow. I slept little, but have seldom enjoyed a more pleasant or refreshing night's rest. Daylight arrived without our having been disturbed by anything more formidable than a mouse, or something like it, which found its way under my blanket, and for a moment startled me by rubbing against my throat.

∞

Frederick Law Olmsted, *A Journey through Texas; or, a Saddle-Trip on the Southwestern Frontier* (1852–57)

BUFFALO BAYOU AND DOWNTOWN HOUSTON FROM THE WEST

Toward the latter end of June, the heat becomes more intense. I had an opportunity of inspecting a thermometrical table, from the middle to the end of this month, which showed a range of temperature from ten o'clock A.M. to four o'clock P.M. between 85 and 93°, and in some instances the mercury rose to 100°. As you advance in the month of July, the heat becomes more oppressive and the atmosphere more sultry. The system now, under long continued heat, begins to lose its tone, and both mind and body sink into a state of debility and indifference. Many seek to overcome this languor by stimulating drinks, which, like most temporary expedients, only aggravate the disease and often lead to the horrors, to settled melancholy, or delirium, and other morbid diseases, which indicate a deranged state of the system and especially the brain. Sickness now begins to show itself in the shape of intermittents, which are marked with no particular violence, but as the system is at this time much over-rated and has lost much of its stamina, they are extremely difficult to eradicate. Those who are attacked in this month are extremely happy if they do not suffer during the whole summer and even winter, and still more so if the disease, in the progress of the season, does not assume a more dangerous type and end in death.

Texas in 1837: An Anonymous, Contemporary Narrative

FROM BUFFALO BAYOU, UNDER INTERSTATE 45

Fishing in Buffalo Bayou at Allen's Landing, downtown Houston

Main Street to the San Jacinto Battlefield

Buffalo Bayou flows in a winding path to the east out of downtown Houston until it reaches its junction with the San Jacinto River, a distance of approximately seventeen miles by air. The serpentine course of the bayou, however, covers almost forty miles between these two points. At roughly the midpoint along this route, Brays Bayou flows in from the south, marking the site of the historic town of Harrisburg.

The start of this stretch, where White Oak Bayou and Buffalo Bayou converge, is marked by Allen's Landing. It was at this point in August of 1836 that the brothers John Kirby Allen and Augustus Chapman Allen, small-time speculators from New York, stepped ashore on their newly acquired tract of land and drew up a plan for the city they envisioned. Historians have questioned whether the spot designated by the city as "Allen's Landing" is in fact the point where the two men first came ashore. Most likely, it's just a good guess as to the exact location. The fact is that the Allen brothers were by no means the only men stepping ashore and looking for the best site for a city along Buffalo Bayou at about that time. Harrisburg, New Washington, Lynchburg, Powhatten, Buffalo, and Hamilton were among the other cities either dreamed about or already under development. Harrisburg, in particular, seemed to have the most advantageous site, located at what was generally agreed to be the head of the bayou's tidewaters.

The Allen brothers had considered buying land and building their city at several sites: Galveston Island, Morgan's Point, and Harrisburg. All these sites either lacked clear titles to the land that the brothers wanted or were tied up in litigation, and time was of the essence. They knew that a major city would emerge along Buffalo Bayou or Galveston Bay, and they made a bold move. They publicly announced that, after careful sounding of Buffalo Bayou, they had determined that the head of tidewaters was not at Harrisburg, as previously thought, but fifteen miles upstream at the junction of White Oak Bayou. On August 30, only five days after they had acquired the site, they took out newspaper advertisements, boldly announcing that "the town of Houston is located at a point on the river which

Main Street bridge
over Buffalo Bayou
at Allen's Landing

must ever command the trade of the richest portion of Texas . . . and when the rich lands of this country shall be settled, a trade will flow to it, making it, beyond all doubt, the great interior commercial emporium of Texas."

Almost immediately, skeptics began to question the Allen brothers' claim that tidewaters flowed all the way to their new town. In January of 1837, compelled to prove that Houston was indeed at the head of navigation on the bayou, the Allen brothers arranged for a small steamboat, the *Laura,* to settle the issue. They persuaded a number of prominent citizens to board the boat at Columbia on the Brazos River and sail up Buffalo Bayou to the new city of Houston. Among the distinguished men on board for that trip were John Kirby Allen himself, Mosely Baker, a hero of the battle of San Jacinto, and Francis Richard Lubbock, who would one day be governor of Texas.

No boat had ever traveled Buffalo Bayou above Harrisburg, and it took the *Laura* three days to travel the roughly fifteen miles. All the passengers had to join with the crew in efforts to free the vessel from the logs and snags that blocked virtually every turn of the bayou. Days consisted of hard work for all aboard, but in the evenings everyone went ashore to party and dance with the settlers along the way.

On January 22, 1837, the *Laura* arrived at the site of Houston. Several men, impatient with the slow progress of the trip, had left the day before on a little yawl and sailed upstream, searching for the townsite but passing it. They became stuck in the brush of White Oak Bayou before they turned around, came back downstream, and finally found a single road laid off from the edge of the water. Once ashore, they found a few stakes and footprints. They had discovered Houston.

The *Laura* was the first of many steamers to navigate the waters of Buffalo Bayou. By the 1840s a dozen or more steamboats regularly carried passengers between Galveston and Houston. The journey took about ten hours and cost five dollars for a cabin passenger and fifty cents for a barrel of freight. By all accounts, these early bayou steamboats were strange-looking vessels. One traveler described them as looking like Noah's Ark, but "built of live oak instead of gopher wood." One of the most memorable aspects of the steamboat trips to Houston from Galveston was the passage up the narrow, winding bayou at night. Bonfires were built in huge buckets on each side of the bow to light the way through the dense foliage that grew out from the banks. Travelers would recall the whine of the high-pressure steam engines, the unearthly chants of Negro boatmen, and the howls of animals along the shore.

Today Buffalo Bayou is a totally different stream along the stretch that the *Laura* covered in 1837. By all accounts, the banks of the bayou in those days were lush with vegetation and covered with towering trees. A tangled mass of oaks draped with Spanish moss, flowering plants, and luxuriant undergrowth lined the bayou on both sides. The magnificent *Magnolia grandiflora* stood over it all, huge evergreen trees with white, fragrant blossoms. Only a few traces of that once magnificent beauty remain. The banks of Buffalo Bayou in this area are lined now with refineries, scrap metal yards, industrial plants, and facilities for the manufacturing of plastics, fertilizers, and specialty chemicals. At night, huge barges and tankers glide smoothly and silently along the water, lit not by bonfires but by the glow of a million lights from nearby refineries.

Approximately six miles downstream from Allen's Landing, the bayou takes a sharp bend to the north and

widens into what is known today as the Turning Basin of the Houston Ship Channel. This marks the beginning of the Port of Houston. Wharves, giant storage sheds, and huge elevators line the north side of the bayou. Ocean-going barges and enormous vessels from around the world are docked for loading and unloading their cargo. The Port of Houston ranks first among U.S. ports in foreign tonnage. Over a hundred major petrochemical plants line the banks of the Houston Ship Channel from the Turning Basin all the way to Galveston Bay. Day and night, around the clock and throughout the year, the barges and ships come and go, transporting every imaginable product to and from Houston and the world.

The ship channel flows due east at first, under Loop 610, then under Beltway 8, until it begins to bear to the northeast. The San Jacinto Monument can be seen on the right, on the south side of the bayou, marking the other great historic site on Buffalo Bayou, the San Jacinto Battlefield.

BUFFALO BAYOU, WEST OF THE TURNING BASIN

Buffalo Bayou, east of downtown Houston

PORT OF HOUSTON ON BUFFALO BAYOU

Further on night overtook us as we entered the narrows of Buffalo bayou. It seemed our boat entered with a very tight squeeze. We made very little headway from there to Houston. Captain Sterett had two huge bonfires made, one on each side of the bow of the boat of pine knots. These fires were made in iron baskets, supported on iron rods attached to the bow, so that the boat in moving along carried its own light. These lights in straight parts of the bayou it lit up for some distance, but when the boat would have to make short curves in following the winding stream the bow would frequently appear to rest in one bank of the bayou and the stern on the other, and then the lights would make it appear as if we were about to take to the woods. All trace of water was gone until the deck hands with their long poles would, by pushing against the bank, turn the prow of the boat into the stream again. At these times the boat, gliding smoothly and almost without noise along the banks, the torches casting grewsome shadows of the big trees here and there, the thumping of the machinery, the ringing of the bells signaling the engineer to "go ahead" or "reverse," mixed with the wild refrain of the boat hands singing their chorus songs; the darkness and stillness of the night outside, except when broken by the occasional howl of some wild animal, made one feel as if he were wandering in dreamland.

∞

Sixty Years on the Brazos: The Life and Letters of Dr. John Washington Lockhart, 1824–1900 (1839)

PORT OF HOUSTON AND BUFFALO BAYOU AT NIGHT

BARGES AND REFINERIES ON BUFFALO BAYOU

It was about two o'clock in the afternoon of a bright frosty day, that we put ourselves on board the Houston steamer—Captain Kelsey. She was a small vessel, and drew but little water, a circumstance very necessary in these small rivers. The American river steamers differ very much in appearance from those to which an European eye is accustomed. They have the appearance of wooden houses, built upon a large raft; there is a balcony or verandah, and on the roof is what is called a hurricane deck, where *gentleman* passengers walk and smoke. On the occasion of our taking our passage both ladies and gentlemen's cabin were quite full, and I therefore preferred spending the evening in the balcony in spite of the cold. I had many kind offers of civility, but I could not help being amused at the terms in which some of them were couched. The question addressed to me of "do you liquor, ma'am" was speedily followed by the production of a tumbler of *egg-noggy* . . .

We dined soon after our arrival on board and found every body very orderly and civil; certainly there was a strange mixture of ranks, but this made it more amusing to a stranger. The ladies, during dinner, were very silent, though the noise I had heard them making in their own cabin, five minutes, before was deafening. The supper consisted of alternate dishes of boiled oysters, and beef steaks, of which there was plenty, and the latter disappeared in marvelously quick time between the strong jaws of the Texas gentlemen. I confess to preferring meat which has been kept somewhat more than an hour, especially in frosty weather. On one occasion our dinner was delayed for some time, while the cook went on shore and "shot a beef."

∞

Matilda Charlotte (Jesse) Fraser Houstoun, *Texas and the Gulf Coast of Mexico; or, Yachting in the New World* (1842)

The town of Lynchburg presently came into view. It is located on the right bank of the San-Jacinto, a short distance below the point where Buffalo Bayou empties into the river. This new-born city consists of a few houses, and some ship yards are already in operation. I saw a schooner under repair, and everything pointed to commercial activity for which nature has prepared great resources. The steamer stopped only long enough to take on a few passengers. General Houston, ex-President of the Republic, was of the number. That evening we visited San-Jacinto battlefield with him, on the banks of Buffalo Bayou, where the boat had taken us. As navigation became difficult and dangerous in the dark, the boat was moored to some large trees, on the left bank of the bayou, and the travelers arranged to spend the night as best they could. The crew jumped ashore, set some trees ablaze, and lay around the fire. As for me, I went back aboard, after my little venture to the battleground, which I had found still strewn with the skeletons of men and horses.

Frédéric Leclerc, *Texas and Its Revolution* (1838)

FISHING AT LYNCHBURG

San Jacinto Monument and Park

After crossing the Trinity River we had a disagreeable time crossing the bay. It had been raining two days and nights. There was a bayou to cross over which there was no bridge, and the only way to pass was to go three miles through the bay to get around the mouth of the bayou. There were guide-posts to point out the way, but it was very dangerous. If we got near the mouth of the bayou there was quicksand. If the wind rose the waves rolled high. The bayou was infested with alligators. A few days before our family arrived at the bay a Mr. King was caught by one and carried under water. He was going east with his family. He swam his horses across the mouth of the bayou, and then he swan back to the west side and drove the cart into the bay. His wife and children became frightened, and he turned back and said he would go up the river and wait for the water to subside. He got his family back on land, and swam the bayou to bring back the horses. He had gotten nearly across with them, when a large alligator appeared. Mrs. King first saw it above water and screamed. The alligator struck her husband with its tail and he went under water, There were several men present, and they fired their guns at the animal, but it did no good. It was not in their power to rescue Mr. King. The men waited several days and then killed a beef, put a quarter on the bank, fastened it with a chain, and then watched it until the alligator came out, when they shot and killed it. This happened several days before the battle.

∞

"The Reminiscences of Mrs. Dilue Harris"

. . . We crossed the San Jacinto the next morning and stayed until late in the evening on the battle field. Both armies were camped near. General Santa Anna had been captured. There was great rejoicing at the meeting of friends. Mr. Leo Roark was in the battle. He had met his mother's family the evening before. He came to the ferry just as it landed, and it was like seeing a brother. He asked mother to go with him to the camp to see General Santa Anna and the Mexican prisoners. She would not go, because, as she said, she was not dressed for visiting; but she gave sister and me permission to go to the camp. I had lost my bonnet crossing Trinity Bay and was compelled to wear a table cloth again. It was six weeks since we had left home, and our clothes were very much dilapidated. I could not go to see the Mexican prisoners with a table cloth tied on my head for I knew several of the young men. I was on the battle field of San Jacinto the 26th of April, 1836. The 28th was the anniversary of my birth. I was eleven years old.

We stayed on the battle field several hours. Father was helping with the ferry boat. We visited the graves of the Texans that were killed in the battle, but there were none of them that I knew. The dead Mexicans were lying around in every direction.

Mother was very uneasy about Uncle James Wells, who was missing. Mr. Roark said uncle had been sent two days before the battle with Messrs. Church Fulcher, and Wash Secrest to watch General Cos. They had gone to Stafford's Point, and were chased by the Mexicans and separated. Father and Secrest returned before the battle. Mr. Roark says the burning of Vince's bridge prevented several of the scouts from getting back.

Father worked till the middle of the afternoon helping with the ferry boat, and then he visited the camp. He did not see General Santa Anna, but met some old friends he had known in Missouri. We left the battle field late in the evening. We had to pass among the dead Mexicans, and father pulled one out of the road, so we could get by without driving over the body, since we could not go around it. The prairie was very boggy, it was getting dark, and there were now twenty or thirty families with us. We were glad to leave the battle field, for it was a grewsome sight. We camped that night on the prairie, and we could hear the wolves howl and bark as they devoured the dead.

∞

"The Reminiscences of Mrs. Dilue Harris"

LYNCHBURG TO THE GULF OF MEXICO

Maps of the Texas Gulf Coast show a series of rivers—the Sabine, Neches, Trinity, San Jacinto, and Brazos—all flowing from inland Texas in a southward direction into the Gulf of Mexico. These rivers all meander, but follow roughly parallel paths from the northwest to the southeast as they bring water from the higher elevations to empty into the sea.

Across this coastal plain—a product of sixty-five million years of sedimentary erosion from the mountain ranges to the north—only one stream of any size flows in an west-east direction: Buffalo Bayou. Along its route of approximately sixty-five miles, Buffalo Bayou collects the waters of other streams, large and small. White Oak Bayou as well as Brays, Sims, and Greens Bayous all join Buffalo Bayou as it flows past Houston to the east, finally reaching its mouth at its junction with the San Jacinto River.

The exact point of this confluence—where Buffalo Bayou and the San Jacinto River meet—has proven to be a crucial point, not only in the history of Texas and the United States, but in the geological history of Buffalo Bayou as well. Geologists tell us that this is where Buffalo Bayou began.

From radiocarbon tests on soil samples taken deep in the fluvial channel of the bayou, geologists can date the origin of Buffalo Bayou to almost exactly 18,000 years ago. The story they tell of the formation of Buffalo Bayou is not unlike that of other rivers around the world whose courses were determined during periods of "lowstand," when the seas were low due to increased glacial formation.

Water, draining from higher land, begins to collect into streams. The flow of those streams, as they gain water and force, begins to cuts gorges into the surface of the earth as the water moves downward to the nearest sea. Some rivers of the Texas Gulf Coast—most notably the Brazos River—are millions of years old and over time have cut numerous valleys.

The San Jacinto is a relatively new river, probably formed less than a million years ago during a relatively recent lowstand. Buffalo Bayou was definitely incised into the earth's surface just less than 18,000 years ago at the apex of the last ice age. It was formed as a tributary of the San Jacinto River, and its unusual west-east course was probably determined by a subsurface fault in the soft, gumbolike soil of the Beaumont formation.

As the great ice sheets of the Northern Hemisphere began to melt, the level of the seas—and hence the level of the rivers that fed into them—began to rise. Over thousands of years, the deep gorges that the rivers had cut began to fill with sediment and the rivers themselves widened.

As the waters of the San Jacinto River rose, a niche appeared in the land along its westward bank, a tiny crack at first. Then, as water continued to rise, the niche became a short stream, collecting drainage and leading to the river, the tiniest tributary. By what geologists call "headway erosion," this stream—what we now call Buffalo Bayou—cut its way west from its juncture with the San Jacinto River. As it worked its way to the west, it collected drainage from the relatively flat land of the coastal plain all the way back to what is now the town of Katy.

By five thousand years ago, the seas had reached their present level. Bays and lagoons had formed all along the Texas Gulf Coast where the water had risen. The full course of Buffalo Bayou had been cut, and its original point of confluence with the San Jacinto River now lay under the shallow waters of Galveston Bay.

· · ·

The San Jacinto Monument marks the most important historical point along Buffalo Bayou. It was here, in April of 1836, barely four months before the Allen brothers founded the city of Houston, that the Texas army under General Sam Houston, in a battle that lasted less than twenty minutes, surprised and annihilated the Mexican army under Santa Anna. Many Mexican soldiers fled from their encampments along the bayou into the nearby marshes and lagoons, where they were shot by the Texan soldiers.

The victory was not only one of the most decisive battles in history, but a major event in United States and Mexican history. Initially, it gave Texas freedom from Mexico, and it eventually led to the annexation of Texas by the United States, then to the Mexican War, and finally to the acquisition by the United States of over a third of the present area of the country.

Directly north of the monument and battlefield, the San Jacinto River converges with Buffalo Bayou at Lynchburg, the historic site of Nathaniel Lynch's early settlement and ferry. From Lynchburg to the Gulf of Mexico, approximately sixty miles to the southeast, the waterway that carries ships and barges from the Port of Houston to the open sea is known as the Houston Ship Channel. The ship channel crosses a number of small bays, lined on both sides by facilities of the Port of Houston, turns to the south past Morgan's Point, and then heads across the shallow expanse of Galveston Bay. The barges and ships that follow the channel to the sea must wind their way around Red Fish Bar, then pass the north end of Galveston Island and the south tip of Bolivar Peninsula before reaching the Gulf of Mexico.

One hundred and seventy-five years ago Nicholas Clopper's schooner, the *Little Zoe,* sat at anchor in the waters of the gulf, "in sight of land" and probably just outside what is now the Houston Ship Channel. Clopper and his sons were waiting for favorable winds and calm seas before they embarked on their journey across Galveston Bay and up Buffalo Bayou.

Today the captains of huge tankers and seagoing barges from around the world set anchor almost daily in the same water. Across the flat, marshy landscape of the Bolivar Peninsula or from the eastern tip of Galveston Island they can be seen, lined up in single file, waiting their turn to bring the world to Texas.

FISHING IN THE SAN JACINTO RIVER AT LYNCHBURG

Marshlands and barges on the Houston Ship Channel

Marshlands along Galveston Bay, Galveston County

To Presidio San Luis de Ahumada or Orcoquizac.

On the 9th we traveled ten leagues principally south, although the road makes a semi-circle to avoid the lagoon formed by the Trinidad river, which lay two leagues to our right all day. . . .

The map I drew shows the size of this presidio . . . It is situated in the country belonging to the Orcoquizac Indian nation which is one league from the Gulf of Mexico in an easterly direction and five leagues on the south from the mouth of the [Trinity] river. After it flows a quarter of a league west of the presidio it becomes very wide and deep, its low banks damming it up. A sandbank closes its mouth and stops its flow. Thus the entire country is full of lagoons which prevent one from traveling along its banks. . . .

The garrison of this presidio consists of a cavalry company of thirty-one men, including captain, lieutenant, and sergeant. Its annual cost is 13,245 pesos. Nine hundred pesos is the allotment of the two Franciscan friars who minister to the troop and the adjoining mission of the Nuestra Señora de la Luz. Here the same conditions prevail as at the preceding missions. I therefore consider this presidio useless since it does not serve the missions. . . . We can sacrifice a certain Monsieur Lampin who traded in a few hides on that uninhabitable coast, secure in this belief that no nation would attempt to form a colony there . . . It is very unhealthy and in the midst of lagoons which make communication impossible with any other of our settlements. For this reason as well as poor management, those unhappy people are compelled to live the greater part of the year on roots called sweet potatoes, medlars, nuts, plums, and chestnuts smaller than those of Spain, and other wild fruits. This is the customary diet of those natives whose laziness makes them content with it rather than trouble to hunt deer and bear, of which there is an abundance. They depend, for their final recourse, upon the lagoon, where there are many fish which they harpoon. Alligators also abound there. The Indians play with them, catching them by the snout and dragging them to shore where they kill them.

∞

The Frontiers of New Spain: Nicolas de Lafora's Description, 1766–1768

I entered Texas by the San-Jacinto. Nothing was more striking than the contrast between the virgin solitudes through which we were traveling and the steamboat on which we rode. On both sides of the river was savage nature, her uncultivated prairies covered with tall grass, no trace of man, his works, or his needs; but on this river, constantly churned by our powerful machine, was modern ingenuity represented by one of its most marvelous creations, industry changing the face of the globe, civilization summed up in one of its most energetic instruments! . . . Here and there in the midst of the endless prairie washed by the San-Jacinto were to be seen clusters of great trees, like tiny islands in the sea of grass. Occasionally the forest would advance to the edge of the river and follow it in all its meanderings. Vegetation is as varied as it is luxuriant in this part of Texas. The *taxodium distichum*, *juniperus*, and pines, which I had first noticed, were succeeded as we progressed up the San-Jacinto, by magnificent groves of oaks, mingling with enormous magnolias. Beautiful laurels were seen also from time to time, and the country side, though not hilly, was neither monotonous nor depressing. . . . as we went inland from the coast, the temperature went noticeably upwards; the air was very calm, and the silence of the wilderness was broken only by the hissing of the steam. . . . Herds of deer would pass in the distance; thousands of birds swept around us; immense flocks of pelicans were willing to be approached without seeming to be the least frightened; and the surface of the water furrowed by the steamer was dotted with ducks and wild geese.

∞

Frédéric Leclerc, *Texas and Its Revolution* (1838)

By the middle of March have about two acres of ground cleared and planted in cane corn beans and a variety of garden vegetables purchase a couple of houses and cut large timber for another—tear down those standing and construct with the whole a raft, consisting of four houses with board and stuff sufficient to roof them—collect our farming utensils kitchen furniture bedding etc and prepare for a voyage of 30 miles on a raft to the mouth of the San Jacinto at Hunter's Point—our league—Dr. Patrick myself and cook Frank compose the crew—first day's sail 1 mile—next day 2 by working hard at the oars frequently against wind and tide—second night endure a thunder storm—very heavy rain—cold and wet through—walking the raft a great part of the night—body ill at east [*sic*]—but mind solacing itself in far distant lands. I go ashore and kill two fine fat turkies—catch a fish weighing about 20 lbs—live well while these last—fourth day we have sunk so that half our deck is under water—meet a canoe bound for Harrisburg send word for speedy assistance—same day meet the Schr. Pomona from Orleans for the same Port Send further intelligence of our *distress.*

Sunday—floating along. Sun beaming down upon us with almost intolerable violence land—our dog discovers a large rattle snake in the high grass—set fire to it—the wind rises and very soon the prairie for a considerable distance is one conflagration forming a truly appalling spectacle! in about half an hour great numbers of crows daws hawks and other carnivorous birds are hovering over this scene of destruction ready to devour the various animals found, ready roasted—a large alligator swims close up to the raft lands among the rushes—attacks our dog which escapes—fire two guns at him without any other effect than to drive him off . . .

∞

"J. C. Clopper's Journal and Book of Memoranda for 1828, Province of Texas"

At the crossing of one of these bayous, we once witnessed a most comical scene. We were returning from a shooting excursion in a light carriage, and were accompanied by an English gentleman on horseback. We had crossed our last bayou in safety, when we found a traveller, going in the contrary direction on foot, waiting patiently for a lift over the water. He was a Frenchman, and his figure was rather an anomaly in these wild regions; he was accoutred in the full costume of l*a jeune France*; long *chevelure*, *pantalons à sous pied*; coat, guiltless of collar, and painted boots: sure "such a man was never formed" to tread the pathless prairies, and how he got there, and who he was, I could not guess, and never have to this day. But there he stood, bowing and shrugging, with a most cat-like horror of wetting his feet. He was evidently most anxiously looking out for an opportunity of crossing the awful looking breakers dry-shod. No sooner did our companion perceive his situation, than he kindly offered to recross the water, provided the Frenchman would mount behind him.

This, however, was sooner said than done; it being no easy matter for a gentleman, evidently not too well skilled in equestrian exercises, to effect a location on the back of a fiery steed, quite unused to carry any extra burden. The cavalier attempted to spring up, *au pantalon étroit*; but it was all in vain; for after each successive effort he found himself stretched on *terra firma*. After many fruitless attempts, he changed his ground, and eventually succeeded in *fixing* himself in front, with his arms clinging closely around our friend's throat. In vain, however, the unfortunate rider, suffering for his philanthropy, implored to be released. "Mais Monsieur," vociferated the Frenchman, in the true spirit of Sinbad's "Old Man of the Sea," "Je suis très bien comme ça." "If you are, I'm not," was the reply; and in a moment, the arms were transferred to the neck of the horse; and thus, with legs dangling, and himself hanging on as if for the bare life, the poor foreigner was safely conveyed across the breakers.

∞

Matilda Charlotte (Jesse) Fraser Houstoun, *Texas and the Gulf Coast of Mexico; or, Yachting in the New World* (1842)

MARSHLANDS AND BAYOU, GALVESTON COUNTY

Leaving Houston, we followed a well-marked road, as far as a bayou, beyond which we entered a settlement of half-a-dozen houses, that, to our surprise, proved to be the town of Harrisburg, a rival (at some distance) of Houston. It is the starting-point of the only railroad yet completed in Texas, extending to Richmond on the Brazos, and has a depth of water in the bayou sufficient for a larger class of boats from Galveston. Houston, however, having ten or fifteen years, and odd millions of dollars, the start, will not be easily overridden. Taking a road here, by direction, which, after two miles, only ran "up a tree," we were obliged to return for more precise information.

At noon, we were ferried over a small bayou by a shining black bundle of rags, and instructed by her as follows:

"Yer see dem two tall pine in de timber ober dar cross de parara, yandar. Yer go right straight da, and da yer'll see de trail somewar. Dat ar go to Lynchburg. Lor! I'se nebber been da—don'no wedder's ary house or no—don'no wedder's ary deep byoo or no—reckon yer can go, been so dry."

Two miles across the grass we found the pines and a trail, which continually broke into cattle-paths, but, by following the general course, we duly reached San Jacinto, a city somewhat smaller than Harrisburg, laid out upon the edge of the old battle-field.

∞

Frederick Law Olmsted, *A Journey through Texas; or, a Saddle-Trip on the Southwestern Frontier* (1857)

MARSHLANDS AND POWER PLANT, GALVESTON COUNTY

Monday, May 8 [1837].—Today we hoisted anchor, bound for Houston; after grounding a few times, we reached Red Fish Bar, distant twelve miles, where we found several American schooners and one brig. It blew hard all night, and we were uncomfortable.

Tuesday, May 9.—We left Red Fish Bar with the *Crusader* and the gig, and with a fair wind proceeded rapidly. Soon we came up to the new-born town of New Washington, owned mostly by Swartwout, the collector of customs of New York. We passed several plantations; and the general appearance of the country was more pleasing than otherwise. About noon, we entered Buffalo Bayou, at the mouth of the San Jacinto River, and opposite the famous battle-ground of the same name. Proceeding smoothly up the bayou, we saw abundance of game, and after traveling some twenty miles stopped at the house of a Mr. Batterson. This bayou is usually sluggish, deep, and bordered on both sides with a trip of woods not exceeding a mile in depth. . . . It was here today that I found the Ivory-Billed Woodpecker in abundance, and secured several specimens. . . . It rained and lightened, and we passed the night at Mr. Batterson's.

∞

John James Audubon, Journal

Houston Ship Channel and refineries, Galveston County

Harrisburg is laid out on the west side of this bayou just below its junction with Bray's bayou—it is yet in the woods consisting of 6 or 8 houses scatteringly situated—the timber consisting principally of tall pine and oaks so excludes the prairie breezes as to render the Summer's heat almost intolerable, but this can be the case but for a short time—being situated at the head of navigation without any local cause for unhealthiness and surrounded by a vast quantity of timber which in this country must prove immensely valuable there is only wanted a population a little more dense and a few capitalists of enterprise and energy to render it one of the most important towns in the colony—here then we safely landed on friday the 4th. January 1828—we pass the winter in a small log pen our fire in one corner—have a great deal of rain for five or six weeks—no snow and very little frost—in all as to weather the most delightful winter I ever lived through. Shoulder our axes and build a fine large warehouse with a shed dining room—move across Bray's bayou into it—now feel ourselves comfortable—sitting in our own house—the work of our own hands and as the N. Western winds blow cool and chill encircling a large log heap at evening hour as a band of youthful brothers and as the spiral flames dispelled the gloom of night, so would we feel our cares our Secret griefs dissipated by the genial influence of social converse. "Home! sweet home! receptacle of each fond tender tie that binds us to existence" this would be our theme. The winter passed away without the melioration of gentle woman's converse—there are it is true several married women—but these are seemingly of as rough a mould as their uncultivated and disagreeably rustic partners there are but two unmarried females in the quarter, to me altogether, unpossessed of the *winning* graces of which their sex is so Susceptible. Several evenings the Doctr and myself made efforts to soothe "the savage breasts" with "concord of sweet sounds," but we found little or no "music in their souls" . . .

∞

"J. C. Clopper's Journal and Book of Memoranda for 1828, Province of Texas"

HOUSTON SHIP CHANNEL, SOUTH OF HIGHWAY 146

Saturday evening four or five of us went ashore with our guns and lay till morning in the soft grass—not knowing that it was Sunday we rambled about shooting at geese ducks and other waterfowl of the country—which collect here in innumerable multitudes every morning to feed on marine substances that are left on the beach by the tide Shot some fine large red fish which with our fowl and oysters afforded our craving appetites a banquet that was most exquisitely delicious and savoury—not able to get our vessel off to day go on shore again in the evening—kindle a large fire of drift wood—none growing upon this point of the island—step a little distance to a small bayou where we gather loads of oysters—roast them and feast till feasting is a labour and we are invited to repose by "tired Nature: sweet restorer—balmy sleep." Monday morning see deer on the island—out shooting again—in the evening at flood tide succeed in hauling out into deep water—lay at anchor till tuesday morning—favourable breeze from the South hoist Sail and pursue the western channel running on the left of Pelican island, so called from the vast number of that species of bird that are continually seen on and about it—sailed many miles through water of five feet depth our schooner drawing upward of four and a half . . .

∾

"J. C. Clopper's Journal and Book of Memoranda for 1828,
Province of Texas"

Bolivar Peninsula and ships on the Houston Ship Channel

Jany 2nd (should be 3rd) [1828]—Went
ashore this morning and planted some orange and Lemon
seeds, then returned on board and weighed anchor,
unfurled our canvass and sailed up the river for Harrisburgh about 30 miles up, by water. Doct. Hunter served us
as Pilot to lynch's ferry about ten miles from his residence.
we hove to at the ferry and lay at anchor an hour or two.
this ferry is at the junction of the Sanjacenta and Rio Buffalo Rivers, the river is about 150 yards wide, though we
found about six fathom water there and from the mast
head had in view one of the richest and most beautiful
landscapes that the eye of man e'er saw. here we left the
Sanjacenta and sailed up the Rio Buffalo 20 miles to the
City of Harrisburgh. the Rio Buffalo is a beautifully meandering river, from sixty to an hundred yards wide and deep
enough for schooner or Steam Boat navigation. the tide
ebbs and flows once in twenty four hours at Harrisburgh
and rises from six to twelve inches. Harrisburgh is situated
at the junction of Buffalo Bayou and Brays Bayou, which
form the Rio Buffalo River. We arrived at Harrisburgh on
the 4th of Jany 1828.

∞

Edward N. Clopper, *An American Family: Its Ups and Downs*
through Eight Generations from 1650 to 1880

Fishing in Galveston Bay

You will never get a just idea of this beautiful land. I already begin to feel. . . . that here I wish to fix & never move. Everybody here is animated, gay & busy—full of hopes & plans. . . .

Passed new Washington & the house of Col: Morgan—where oranges are growing in abundance and perfection. San Jacinto Bay is so lovely we could do nothing but exclaim with expressions of admiration. Bower & lake & wood & lawn alternately. Col: Meads place in all beauty was nothing to it. Talk not of the beauty of Kentucky. it is winter. From the hurricane deck have surveyed the Battle ground of San Jacinto Col: Hockly & Judge Franklin, who were actors in those scenes, described & pointed out the position of the armies, each spot, with the lovely lake that buried so many Mexicans.

∞

Letters of an Early American Traveller, Mary Austin Holley: Her Life and Her Works, 1784–1846

GALVESTON BAY AND THE HOUSTON SHIP CHANNEL

GALVESTON BAY AND THE HOUSTON SHIP CHANNEL

It will not be three weeks till tomorrow since we left you and we have been more than a day lying to at this place, waiting for them to discharge freight into a smaller boat along side, in which we proceed to Houston in a few hours. . . . We have an opportunity of surveying this beautiful Bay at leisure, sitting on the guards on the upper deck, watching the sea-gulls in their gambols; or the less poetical sloops & schooners, in all directions, at anchor, or under sail, besides a goodly number lying high and dry on shore, cast up by the late gale. . . . The weather is most charming. The sun shining, & the Heavens & the sea—the glittering sea—the most perfect cerulean. It is pure delight: remember it is almost Christmas, & a north wind. But to go on—Skiffs, & little sailboats glistening in the sun, are all over the waters. How beautiful it looks. . . . I hope Destiny is driving me on to some good end. I *feel* that something will come of it.

∽

Letters of an Early American Traveller, Mary Austin Holley: Her Life and Her Works, 1784–1846

GALVESTON BAY AND THE HOUSTON SHIP CHANNEL

Dec: 18th [1827] . . .

Thursday morning feel a return of appetite feel a freshness in the breeze—the sea is of a green cast—about 9 o'clock the joyful cry of land is echoed round the deck   strain the eye and discern the breakers at the shore—great flocks of geese and ducks fly over us . . . Saw the sun as he appeared in the act of engulphing himself— shortly after the lovely star of evening gracefully descended the horizon after him and bathed her golden locks in the western tides; . . . the breeze was bland and the surface of the waters unruffled—there was a magnificence in this scenery, an imposing grandeur that seemed to rivet the soul and interest it to exercise all its faculties in contemplation of Him who arrayed them in all their splendour and gave to each his mighty energies—there was a correspondent calmness on the mind—all was quietude . . .

∞

"J. C. Clopper's Journal and Book of Memoranda for 1828, Province of Texas"

EARLY TRAVELERS TO TEXAS

JOHN JAMES AUDUBON traveled through the forests and along the rivers of the American wilderness for several decades of the early nineteenth century, patiently observing and meticulously drawing the birds and animals that had become his passion. His published volume of exquisitely rendered and unfailingly accurate prints, *The Birds of America,* has been called perhaps the greatest gift of art to science in all of history. Drawn to Texas by its vast, unspoiled wilderness and the huge variety of birds to be found there, Audubon traveled up Buffalo Bayou to the town of Houston in the spring of 1837. Along the way he made numerous accounts in his journal of the bayou, the birds and the landscape along it, and life in the newly founded town. His journal of the trip, reconstructed from existing fragments and letters, was published in Samuel Wood Geiser's *Naturalists of the Frontier,* 2nd ed. (Dallas: Southern Methodist University Press, 1948).

∞

J. C. CLOPPER was the son of Nicolas Clopper, who lived in Cincinnati, Ohio, when in 1820 he acquired land in the Province of Texas for speculation and ranching. In 1827 he set out via steamboat with his sons, Joseph (J. C.), Andrew, and Edward, to inspect his newly acquired property and to make preparations to settle there. Joseph's diary of that trip, published as "J. C. Clopper's Journal and Book of Memoranda for 1828, Province of Texas" in the *Quarterly of the Texas State Historical Association* 13 (1909), includes some of the earliest descriptions

of Buffalo Bayou and the Galveston Bay area. EDWARD CLOPPER wrote his own account of a return trip to Texas in the following year, 1828, and included it in his book *An American Family* (Cincinnati, 1950).

∞

GUSTAV DRESEL, son of an affluent German wine merchant, set out for the New World in 1837 at the age of only nineteen. Educated in a classical German high school and then a business college, Dresel aimed, by his travels, to round out his training as a businessman as well as to satisfy his longing for adventurous travel. He spent more than two years headquartered in Houston, from August of 1838 until the summer of 1841. A German version was published in 1922 and then later published in English as *Gustav Dresel's Houston Journal: Adventures in North America and Texas, 1837–1841* (Austin: University of Texas Press, 1954), translated and edited from the German manuscript by Max Freund.

∞

DILUE ROSE HARRIS arrived at Matagorda, Texas, in April of 1833 along with her father, mother, brother, and sister, after a harrowing two-week journey across the Gulf of Mexico from New Orleans. After a brief stay in Harrisburg, flooding and the loss of crops caused the family to move fifteen miles west to a homestead on the Brazos River. In 1839 she married Ira S. Harris, from Jefferson County, New York. Her father, Dr. Pleasant W. Rose, kept a daily journal. The original journal was destroyed, but Harris had previously copied parts of the journal, adding her own recollections, which blend indistinguishably into the manuscript published as "The Reminiscences of Mrs. Dilue Harris" in the *Quarterly of the Texas State Historical Association* 4 (1900–1901).

∞

"Diary of a Young Man in Houston, 1838," the daily journal of JOHN HUNTER HERNDON, is one of the only surviving diaries that record more than a brief visit to Houston in its earliest years. Herndon graduated in both arts and law from Transylvania College in Lexington, Kentucky, and came to Houston two years after the founding of the city. In his four-month-long journal, he describes day-to-day life in a tough and violent town. His matter-of-fact accounts of criminals whipped at the post, lynchings, murders, and people freezing to death are interwoven with observations about the more attractive young women in town. Herndon eventually married and settled in Texas, where he practiced law and dabbled in politics. Herndon's diary was edited by Andrew Forest Muir and published in the *Southwestern Historical Quarterly* 53 (1950).

∞

Born and reared in New Haven, Connecticut, MARY AUSTIN HOLLEY met her cousin, the impresario and founder of the Austin Colony of Texas, Stephen F. Austin, while he was attending in school in Connecticut. After her brother, Henry Austin, joined Stephen and settled in Texas, she communicated with them and land was reserved for her on Galveston Bay. She first traveled to Texas in 1831, after which she wrote *Texas, Observations: Historical, Geographical and Descriptive in a Series of Letters* (Austin: Overland Press, 1981). First published in 1833, this was the first "travel book" on Texas to reach the market. Holley returned to Texas in 1835. Her journal of that trip, published as *Letters of an Early American Traveller* (Dallas: Southwest Press, 1933), also provides an enduring record of early Texas life.

∞

MATILDA CHARLOTTE (JESSE) FRASER HOUSTOUN was an aristocratic Englishwoman whose literary family counted among its friends such world-famous figures as the poet William Wordsworth and the naturalist Charles Darwin. In 1842 she set sail for Texas with her husband, a former army officer, in their 200-ton private schooner, the *Dolphin*. She had prepared herself for the trip by reading a number of books, including Tocqueville's *Democracy in America* and Charles Dickens' account of his journey to America. The Houstouns' trip, described in her book *Texas and the Gulf of Mexico; or, Yachting in the New World* (Austin: Taylor, 1991), may have been related to British ambitions regarding the Republic of Texas, but Houstoun's vivid and often humorous descriptions focused on the people, the land itself, the wildlife, and the flora.

∞

EDWARD KING was only twenty-four years old when he and his colleague, James Wells Champney, were hired by *Scribner's Monthly* to travel the entire American South and prepare a report on social and economic conditions there. King and Champney, an illustrator, traveled all of 1873 and the spring and summer of 1874 on the project. They covered more than 25,000 square miles and visited nearly every city and town of any importance in the southern states. First published in 1875, *The Great South* (Baton Rouge: Louisiana State University Press, 1972) includes a lengthy chapter on King's visit to Texas, including Houston. Highly regarded today for his extraordinary perception and learned prose, King went on to write nine books dealing with European subjects and the American South.

∞

From 1766 to 1768 NICOLAS DE LAFORA, a Spanish map maker, accompanied the expedition of the Marqués de Rubí along the Camino Real from Mexico across Texas to Louisiana.

His report to his king, published as *The Frontiers of New Spain: Nicolas de Lafora's Description, 1766–1768* (Berkeley, Calif.: Quivira Society, 1958), is the oldest surviving description of south and southeast Texas. In it, he concluded that the whole country was "not worth one year's allotment of funds" from His Majesty's treasury and recommended, among other things, the extermination of the native Indians and the abandonment of almost all of the Spanish missions in Texas.

∞

Like so many Europeans of the late nineteenth century, FRÉDÉRIC LECLERC was drawn to Texas by an irresistible attraction to exotic, faraway lands. The young French physician made his own adventurous trip to the western frontier of America in 1838, just two years after the founding of Houston. His descriptions of the landscape of Texas and his keen insights into the emerging social and political scene there—first published in 1840 and then in an English translation as *Texas and Its Revolution* (Houston: Anson Jones Press, 1950)—were accepted as authoritative in France at the time.

∞

Sixty Years on the Brazos (Waco: Texian Press, 1967) is a summary of the life of JOHN WASHINGTON LOCKHART. Lockhart came to Texas with his family at the age of sixteen. Traveling up Buffalo Bayou by steamer in 1839, they stopped briefly in Houston, then hired ox-carts to carry them across the muddy prairie to Washington-on-the-Brazos, where they settled. Washington attained financial independence at an early age, enabling him to travel frequently. His recollections of early Houston and his night passage up Buffalo Bayou from Galveston are among the most vivid and memorable descriptions of that time and place.

∞

FRANCIS RICHARD LUBBOCK came to Texas in 1836 to search for his younger brother, Thomas S. Lubbock, who had come to Texas to join the revolution. He went into business in Houston and, at the age of twenty-two, was appointed comptroller of the Republic of Texas by Sam Houston. In 1946, for seventy-five cents an acre, he bought a four-hundred-acre ranch south of the bayou six miles from Houston. In 1861 he was elected governor of Texas. His recorded his personal experiences in "business, war, and politics" in his autobiography, *Six Decades in Texas* (Austin, 1900).

∞

The diary attributed to A. W. MOORE was more likely written by his brother T. C. Moore, a Mississippi planter. Thomas C. Moore was looking for a good location to settle when he crossed the Mississippi River on horseback in 1846, headed for Texas. After first setting up his household in Bastrop County, he moved to Fayette County and ran a large plantation. He later told his grandson that he wrote much of the "day book" while sitting cross-legged on his horse or by the light of his campfire. The diary was published as "A Reconnoissance in Texas in 1846" in the *Southwestern Historical Quarterly* 30 (1927).

∞

Z. N. MORRELL was a nineteen-year-old ordained Baptist minister from Tennessee when he took "Texas fever" and decided to join his old buddies Sam Houston and Davy Crockett. After swimming his team of horses across Buffalo Bayou in 1837, he changed his wagoner clothes for those of a preacher and set out to preach the first sermon delivered in the newly founded city of Houston. He recounted his subsequent thirty-five years as an itinerant preacher in southern Texas in his autobiography, *Flowers and Fruits from the Wilderness* (Boston: Gould and Lincoln, 1872).

∞

Before coming to Texas, FREDERICK LAW OLMSTED traveled extensively in New England, Canada, China, and Europe.

His first book, *Walks and Talks of an American Farmer in England* (1852), was widely read. Commissioned to write articles for the *New York Times*, Olmsted made extensive tours throughout the southern United States from 1852 to 1857. One of the products of this travel was *A Journey through Texas; or, a Saddle-Trip on the Southwestern Frontier* (New York: Dix, Edwards & Co., 1857), in which Olmsted described aspects of the landscape and life of Texas at that time.

∞

FERDINAND VON ROEMER was the author of the first monograph on Texas geology. Born and educated in Germany, with a Ph.D. degree in paleontology, he came to Texas in 1845 and explored from Galveston as far north as Dallas. Originally published in German in 1849, his book *Texas* (San Antonio, 1935) describes both the physical appearance of the region and the German immigration to Texas.

∞

GASPAR JOSÉ DE SOLÍS, a Franciscan missionary, traveled through Texas in 1767 and 1768, just months after Lafora's visit. The purpose of his journey was an inspection of the Texas missions. His account, published in English as "Diary of a Visit of Inspection of the Texas Missions Made by Fray Gaspar José de Solís in the Year 1767–68" in the *Southwestern Historical Quarterly* 35 (1931), includes a detailed description of the rivers, lakes, and landscape of Texas at the time.

∞

HORACE D. TAYLOR first came to Houston in 1838, two and a half years after the battle of San Jacinto. *Early Days on the Bayou, 1838–1890: The Life and Letters of Horace Dickinson Taylor* by Ellen

Robbins Red (Waco: Texian Press, 1986) gives a first-hand account of the daily life of the young cotton merchant, who eventually served as mayor of Houston.

∞

Perhaps the earliest written account of the Republic of Texas is "Notes on Texas," written by an unknown person and printed in 1838 and 1839 in *Hesperian* magazine. The anonymous author arrived on Galveston Island in March of 1837, before the city of Galveston had been founded, and spent the next six months in the new republic. His vivid images of life in Texas were eventually edited by Andrew Forest Muir and published as *Texas in 1837: An Anonymous, Contemporary Narrative* (Austin: University of Texas Press, 1958).

∞

The identity of the author of *A Visit to Texas in 1831* is not known. It is known, however, that he came to Texas in early March of 1831 to learn what kind of property he had bought from land promoters in New York. Unfortunately, he quickly concluded—along with many others—that his land scrip was worthless and that he had been swindled. Nevertheless, he became enamored of Texas as he traveled through it, and the book stands as one of the finest pieces of descriptive writing of its kind done at that time. If you wanted to read about the primitive wilderness that was Texas in the 1830s, you could choose either Mary Austin Holley's *Texas* or this book, both of which were widely circulated and often quoted. The book was first published in 1834, followed by a second edition in 1836. The third edition is edited by Robert S. Gray (Houston: Cordovan Press, 1975).

Acknowledgments

I would like to express my deepest appreciation to those who enabled me to undertake and complete the work that culminated in this book. In the beginning, when I had little more than an idea, Barry Abrams, Bob Scott, and Susan Bickley responded to my initial efforts to find support for the photography. Their law firm, Abrams, Scott, Bickley, made it possible for me to continue the work. For their patronage in the very earliest stage of the project, I am more grateful than I can express.

As the project progressed, I also received important financial support from American General Corporation, from Harry Zuber, and from the Humanities Division of Rice University. I want to thank them, as well as Jim Jard and Metro National Corporation, for helping me in countless ways as this project came to fruition.

Photographing Buffalo Bayou and the Houston Ship Channel for the five-year duration of the project was an adventure that I remember with appreciation for the many people who assisted me in important ways. It was Don Green who first put me in a canoe and pointed the way to Buffalo Bayou, and it was Don who invited me to come one summer evening and listen to Janet Wagner, as she talked about the history of Buffalo Bayou. Her authoritative, mesmerizing account of the bayou and its place in the history of our city was deeply inspiring. Terry Hershey, who is widely known as the woman who saved Buffalo Bayou, was also a source of much knowledge and inspiration. I thank her both for her hospitality and her sharing of the voluminous files that she has assembled on issues related to Buffalo Bayou.

I thank Will Howard, librarian at the Texas Room of the Houston Public Library, and all his staff, who patiently and expertly assisted me as I researched the history of early travelers to Texas. Nothing that I found in my research was more inspiring or more helpful than the books of Marilyn McAdams Sibley. Her *Port of Houston: A History* and *Travelers in Texas, 1761–1860* provided both the foundation for my research and the inspiration to combine contemporary photographs with historical accounts of early travelers.

I am grateful to three of my colleagues at Rice University for their help: Professor John Anderson of the Department of Geology gave me an authoritative and clear summary of the geological history of Buffalo Bayou, Professor Karen Broker of the Department of Art and Art History lent a guiding hand as I sketched my simple maps of the bayou, and Professor John Boles of the History Department pointed me to important accounts of early Texas travelers that have come to light in very recent years.

Greg Curtis was among the first to see my initial attempts at structuring the book, and he offered ideas that proved critical in shaping the final product.

For their generous grant that funded the production of this book, I want to express my gratitude to the Wortham Foundation, Inc.

Finally, I want to thank Ron Tyler, Director of the Texas State Historical Association, and George Ward, Director of Publications, for their enthusiasm, their many valuable suggestions, and their careful editing and production of the book.